MICHIGAN LIMITED LIABILITY COMPANY ACT
2015 Edition

Updated through January 1, 2015

Michigan Legal Publishing Ltd.
QUICK DESK REFERENCE SERIES™

© 2014, 2015 Michigan Legal Publishing Ltd.
Grand Rapids, Michigan

Academic and bulk discounts available at
www.michlp.com

No claim to copyright of any government works. While we make every effort to ensure this text is accurate, there is no guarantee that the rules and statutes in this publication are the latest and most up-to-date. Accordingly, this text is for educational purposes only and should not be considered legal advice.

WE WELCOME YOUR FEEDBACK: info@michlp.com

ISBN-13: 978-1505889130
ISBN-10: 1505889138

Table of Contents

MICHIGAN LIMITED LIABILITY COMPANY ACT 1
  Article 1 1
    450.4101 Short title. 1
    450.4102 Definitions. 1
    450.4103 Documents; signatures; requirements. 4
    450.4104 Documents; filing; delivery; endorsement; returning copy; inspection by public; copies admissible in evidence; effective date; form; fees. 4
    450.4105 Failure to promptly file document; notice of refusal to file; judicial review. 6
    450.4106 Documents; inaccurate record or defective execution; certificate of correction; filing; signature; contents; effective date of corrected document. 7
  Article 2 7
    450.4201 Limited liability company; purpose. 7
    450.4202 Limited liability company; formation; filing as evidence that all conditions performed; exception; duration. 8
    450.4203 Articles of organization; contents. 8
    450.4204 Limited liability company; low-profit limited liability company; name; requirements; rights. 9
    450.4204a Limited liability company licensed as nursing home; use of terms. 10
    450.4205 Reserving right to use of name; application; transfer of right. 10
    450.4206 Transacting business under assumed name; certificate; effective period; extension; notice of expiration; rights not created; same name assumed in partnership or joint venture; transfer of assumed name to survivor; use of name by surviving company; assumed name of converted company; certificate of conversion. 11
    450.4207 Maintaining registered office and resident agent; service of process, notice, or demand; appointment of agent; annual statement; service of process by mail. 12
    450.4207a Certificate of good standing. 13
    450.4208 Resident agent; resignation; notice; appointment of successor; termination of appointment. 15
    450.4209 Changing registered office or resident agent; statement; filing; contents; changing business or residence address of resident agent. 15
    450.4210 Limited liability company; powers. 16

450.4211 Validity of action or transfer of property; asserting lack of capacity or power. 16

450.4212 Interest rate; agreement. 16

450.4213 Registered office or principal place of business; documents required to be kept. 17

450.4214 Conflict between articles of organization and operating agreement. 17

450.4215 Operating agreement unenforceable. 17

450.4216 Limited liability company; powers. 17

Article 3 .... **18**

450.4301 Members; contribution. 18

450.4302 Promise by member to contribute; enforcement; obligation to perform; rights of company; compromising obligation; enforcement by creditor of original member's obligation. 18

450.4303 Distribution of assets; allocation; manner; basis. 19

450.4304 Distribution; conditions for receiving. 19

450.4305 Distributions to withdrawing member. 20

450.4306 Distributions; demand, acceptance, and receipt of distribution; form. 20

450.4307 Distributions prohibited under certain situations; exceptions; effect of distribution under subsection (1); remedies available; future payments to withdrawing members; effect of subsection (1) on third party; asserting legal or equitable rights. 20

450.4308 Distribution; violating operating agreement or MCL 450.4307; liability of members or managers; presumption of assent; knowledge of violation; contribution; commencement of proceeding. 23

Article 4 .... **23**

450.4401 Management vested in members. 23

450.4402 Managers; delegation; qualifications; number; notice of delegation. 24

450.4403 Managers; selection; vote; removal; notice. 24

450.4404 Managers; duties; action for failure to perform duties. 25

450.4405 Managers; voting requirements. 26

450.4406 Manager as agent. 26

450.4407 Managers; eliminating or limiting liability; exceptions. 26

450.4409 Manager or agent with interest in company; effect; majority vote by members with no interest in transaction; claims. 27

Article 5 28

450.4501 Members; admission; liability for acts, debts, or obligations. 28

450.4502 Members; voting rights. 29

450.4503 Members; obtaining certain financial statements and tax returns; inspecting and copying records; obtaining other information; formal accounting of company's affairs. 30

450.4504 Membership interest as personal property. 31

450.4505 Membership interest; assignment; liability of assignee; assignor as member; liability of assignor not released. 31

450.4506 Assignee of membership interest; conditions for membership; rights and powers; liability for obligations of assignor. 32

450.4507 Charging membership interest with payment of judgment; rights of judgment creditor; rights and powers of member; charging order as lien on membership interest; section as exclusive remedy. 32

450.4508 Encumbrance against membership interest; effect. ... 33

450.4509 Withdrawal of member; distribution; expulsion. 33

450.4510 Commencement and maintenance of civil suit by company; conditions. 33

450.4511 Investigation of allegations; stay of derivative proceeding. 34

450.4512 Dismissal of derivative proceeding; findings; burden of proof; determination; "disinterested" defined. 34

450.4513 Discontinued or settled derivative proceeding; court approval required; notice; expense. 35

450.4514 Termination of derivative proceeding; court order. ... 36

450.4515 Action in circuit court; grounds; order or grant of relief; "willfully unfair and oppressive conduct" defined. 36

Article 6 37

450.4601 Articles of organization; amendment. 37

450.4602 Articles of organization; conditions requiring amendment. 37

450.4603 Articles of organization; certificate of amendment; filing; contents. 38

450.4604 Restated articles of organization. 38

Article 7 39

450.4701 Domestic limited liability companies; merger; plan. .. 39

450.4702 Merger; approval of plan by members; withdrawal and distribution. 39

450.4703 Plan of merger; execution; certificate; contents and effectiveness. 40

450.4704 Merger; provisions. 40

450.4705 Merger of foreign limited liability companies with domestic limited liability companies; conditions; compliance and liability of surviving company. 41

450.4705a Definitions; merger of domestic limited liability companies with business organizations. 41

450.4706 Abandoning plan of merger; procedure. 44

450.4707 Conversion of domestic partnership or domestic limited partnership to limited liability company. 45

450.4708 Conversion into business organization; requirements; effectiveness of certificate of conversion; foreign business organization as surviving business organization; "business organization" and "entity" defined. 46

450.4709 Conversion of business organization into domestic limited liability company; requirements; effectiveness of certificate of conversion. 49

Article 8 52

450.4801 Dissolution and winding up; conditions. 52

450.4802 Dissolution; decree by circuit court. 52

450.4803 Dissolution; action by attorney general; grounds; other actions not excluded. 52

450.4804 Certificate of dissolution; filing; contents. 53

450.4805 Winding up by managers, members, or circuit court; procedures; right to maintain actions. 54

450.4806 Dissolution; notice to existing claimants; contents; validity of claim not recognized; claims barred under certain conditions; "existing claim" defined; effective date of notice. 54

450.4807 Dissolution; publication of notice; requirements; commencing proceeding to enforce claims; claimants with known existing claims not receiving notice. 55

450.4808 Winding up; distribution of assets; order; filing tax returns and paying tax obligations. 56

Article 9 57

450.4901 Limited liability company; rendering professional services; applicability of article. 57

450.4902 Definitions. 57

450.4903 Professional limited liability company; purpose stated in articles of organization; name. 58

450.4904 Rendering professional services; organization of professional liability company or professional limited liability company; license or legal authorization of persons required. ... 58

450.4905 Professional limited liability company; license required; "employee" explained; effect of act on laws applicable to professional relationship and liabilities; liability for negligent or wrongful acts. 59

450.4906 Disqualification, restriction, or limitation on persons rendering professional service; severing employment and financial interest; noncompliance. 60

450.4907 Professional limited liability company; prohibited activities; exception. 60

450.4908 Sale or transfer of membership interest; restrictions. 61

450.4909 Annual report; filing fee; penalty for late filing. 61

450.4910 Merger; limitation. 63

Article 10 .... **63**

450.5001 Foreign limited liability company; laws of jurisdiction. 63

450.5002 Transacting business; certificate of authority by foreign limited liability company required; application; filing; contents. 63

450.5003 Certificate of authority; issuance; powers, rights, and privileges of foreign limited liability company. 64

450.5004 Certificate of authority; satisfaction of MCL 450.4204 required for issuance. 65

450.5005 Inaccurate application; correcting statement; certificate; exception; survivor of merger; certificate attesting to merger; annual statement. 65

450.5006 Certificate of withdrawal; contents, form, manner, and execution of application. 65

450.5007 Foreign limited liability company; transacting business without certificate of authority. 66

450.5008 Activities not considered to be transacting business in state; applicability of section to other state laws. 68

450.5009 Making or purchasing loans or participation or interest in loans. 69

450.5010 Maintaining action to restrain by attorney general... 69

Article 11 .... **69**

450.5101 Filing fees; use; charges for certifying or copying files or records; dishonored checks; payment by credit card; waiver. 70

450.5102 Effect of actions by legislature. 71

450.5103 Interest as security. 71

450.5200 Effective date. 72

MICHIGAN LIMITED LIABILITY COMPANY ACT

Act 23 of 1993 (as amended)

AN ACT to provide for the organization and regulation of limited liability companies; to prescribe their duties, rights, powers, immunities, and liabilities; to prescribe the powers and duties of certain state departments and agencies; and to provide for penalties and remedies.

The People of the State of Michigan enact:

Article 1

450.4101 Short title.

Sec. 101.

This act shall be known and may be cited as the "Michigan limited liability company act".

450.4102 Definitions.

Sec. 102.

(1) Unless the context requires otherwise, the definitions in this section control the interpretation of this act.
(2) As used in this act:
  (a) "Administrator" means the director of the department or his or her designated representative.
  (b) "Articles of organization" means the original documents filed to organize a limited liability company, as amended or restated by certificates of correction, amendment, or merger, by restated articles, or by other instruments filed or issued under any statute.
  (c) "Constituent" means a party to a plan of merger, including the survivor.
  (d) "Contribution" means anything of value that a person contributes to the limited liability company as a prerequisite for, or in connection with, membership, including cash, property, services performed, or a promissory note or other binding obligation to contribute cash or property, or to perform services.
  (e) "Corporation" or "domestic corporation" means any of the following:

  (i) A corporation formed under the business corporation act, 1972 PA 284, MCL 450.1101 to 450.2098.
  (ii) A corporation existing on January 1, 1973 and formed under another statute of this state for a purpose for which a corporation may be formed under the business corporation act, 1972 PA 284, MCL 450.1101 to 450.2098.
  (iii) A corporation formed under former 1962 PA 192.
(f) "Department" means the department of licensing and regulatory affairs.
(g) "Distribution" means a direct or indirect transfer of money or other property or the incurrence of indebtedness by a limited liability company to or for the benefit of its members or assignees of its members in respect of the members' membership interests.
(h) "Electronic transmission" or "electronically transmitted" means any form of communication that meets all of the following:
  (i) It does not directly involve the physical transmission of paper.
  (ii) It creates a record that may be retained and retrieved by the recipient.
  (iii) It may be directly reproduced in paper form by the recipient through an automated process.
(i) "Foreign limited liability company" means a limited liability company formed under laws other than the laws of this state.
(j) "Foreign limited partnership" means a limited partnership formed under laws other than the laws of this state.
(k) "Limited liability company" or "domestic limited liability company" means an entity that is an unincorporated membership organization formed under this act.
(l) "Limited partnership" or "domestic limited partnership" means a limited partnership formed under the Michigan revised uniform limited partnership act, 1982 PA 213, MCL 449.1101 to 449.2108.
(m) "Low-profit limited liability company" means a limited liability company that has included in its articles of organization a purpose that meets, and that at all times conducts its activities to meet, all of the following requirements:
  (i) The limited liability company significantly furthers the accomplishment of 1 or more charitable or educational purposes described in section 170(c)(2)(B) of the internal revenue code, 26 USC 170, and would not have been formed except to accomplish those charitable or educational purposes.

  (ii) The production of income or appreciation of property is not a significant purpose of the limited liability company. However, in the absence of other factors, the fact that a limited liability company produces significant income or capital appreciation is not conclusive evidence of a significant purpose involving the production of income or the appreciation of property.
  (iii) The purposes of the limited liability company do not include accomplishing 1 or more political or legislative purposes described in section 170(c)(2)(D) of the internal revenue code, 26 USC 170.

(n) "Majority in interest" means a majority of votes as allocated by an operating agreement, or by the statute in the absence of an allocation by operating agreement, and held by members entitled to vote on a matter submitted for a vote by members.

(o) "Manager" or "managers" means a person or persons designated to manage the limited liability company pursuant to a provision in the articles of organization stating that the business is to be managed by or under the authority of managers.

(p) "Member" means a person who has been admitted to a limited liability company as provided in section 501, or, in the case of a foreign limited liability company, a person that is a member of the foreign limited liability company in accordance with the laws under which the foreign limited liability company is organized.

(q) "Membership interest" or "interest" means a member's rights in the limited liability company, including, but not limited to, any right to receive distributions of the limited liability company's assets and any right to vote or participate in management.

(r) "Operating agreement" means a written agreement by the member of a limited liability company that has 1 member, or between all of the members of a limited liability company that has more than 1 member, pertaining to the affairs of the limited liability company and the conduct of its business. The term includes any provision in the articles of organization pertaining to the affairs of the limited liability company and the conduct of its business.

(s) "Person" means an individual, partnership, limited liability company, trust, custodian, estate, association, corporation, governmental entity, or any other legal entity.

(t) "Services in a learned profession" means services rendered by a dentist, an osteopathic physician, a

physician, a surgeon, a doctor of divinity or other clergy, or an attorney-at-law.
(u) "Surviving company", "surviving entity", or "survivor" means the constituent that survives a merger, as identified in the certificate of merger.
(v) "Vote" means an affirmative vote, approval, or consent.

450.4103 Documents; signatures; requirements.

Sec. 103.

(1) One or more persons organizing a limited liability company shall sign the original articles of organization as organizers. The articles shall state the names of the organizers beneath or opposite their signatures.
(2) Any document other than original articles of organization required or permitted to be filed under this act that this act requires be executed on behalf of the domestic limited liability company shall be signed by a manager of the company if management is vested in 1 or more managers, by at least 1 member if management remains in the members, or by any authorized agent of the company. A document required to be executed on behalf of a foreign limited liability company shall be signed by a person with authority to do so under the laws of the jurisdiction of its organization. The document shall state the name of the person signing the document and the capacity in which he or she signs beneath or opposite his or her signature.
(3) A person may sign a document under this section as an authorized agent of a limited liability company. If the authorization is pursuant to a power of attorney, the power of attorney authorizing the signing of the document by the person need not be sworn to, verified, acknowledged, or filed with the administrator. A document signed by a person under this subsection as an authorized agent of a limited liability company shall state the capacity of the person signing the document.

450.4104 Documents; filing; delivery; endorsement; returning copy; inspection by public; copies admissible in evidence; effective date; form; fees.

Sec. 104.

(1) A document required or permitted to be filed under this act shall be submitted by delivering the document to the administrator together with the fees and accompanying documents required by law. The administrator may establish a procedure for accepting delivery of a document submitted under this subsection by

facsimile or other electronic transmission. However, by December 31, 2006, the administrator shall establish a procedure for accepting delivery of a document submitted under this subsection by electronic mail or over the Internet. Beginning January 1, 2007, the administrator shall accept delivery of documents submitted by electronic mail or over the Internet.

(2) If a document submitted under subsection (1) substantially conforms to the requirements of this act, the administrator shall endorse upon it the word "filed" with his or her official title and the date of receipt and of filing, and shall file and index the document or a photostatic, micrographic, photographic, optical disc media, or other reproduced copy in his or her office. If requested at the time of the delivery of the document to his or her office, the administrator shall include the hour of filing in the endorsement on the document.

(3) The administrator shall return a copy of a document filed under subsection (2), or, at his or her discretion, the original, to the person who submitted it for filing. The administrator shall mark the filing date on the copy or original before returning it or, if the document was submitted by electronic mail or over the Internet, may provide proof of the filing date to the person who submitted the document for filing in another manner determined by the administrator.

(4) The records and files of the administrator relating to domestic and foreign limited liability companies shall be open to reasonable inspection by the public. The administrator may maintain the records or files either in their original form or in a photostatic, micrographic, photographic, optical disc media, or other reproduced form.

(5) The administrator may make copies of any documents filed under this act or any predecessor act by a photostatic, micrographic, photographic, optical disc media, or other process, and may destroy the originals of the copied documents. A photostatic, micrographic, photographic, optical disc media, or other reproduced copy certified by the administrator, including a copy sent by facsimile or other electronic transmission, is considered an original for all purposes and is admissible in evidence in like manner as an original.

(6) A document filed under subsection (2) is effective at the time it is endorsed unless a subsequent effective time is set forth in the document that is not later than 90 days after the date of delivery.

(7) The administrator may require that a person submit a document described in subsection (1) on a form prescribed by the administrator.

(8) The administrator shall charge 1 of the following nonrefundable fees if expedited filing of a document by the administrator is requested and the administrator shall retain the revenue collected under this subsection and the department shall use it to carry out its duties required by law:

(a) For any filing that a person requests the administrator to complete within 1 hour on the same day as the day of the request, $1,000.00. The department may establish a deadline by which a person must submit a request for filing under this subdivision.
(b) For any filing that a person requests the administrator to complete within 2 hours on the same day as the day of the request, $500.00. The department may establish a deadline by which a person must submit a request for filing under this subdivision.
(c) Except for a filing request under subdivision (a) or (b), for the filing of any formation or qualification document that a person requests the administrator to complete on the same day as the day of the request, $100.00. The department may establish a deadline by which a person must submit a request for filing under this subdivision.
(d) Except for a filing request under subdivision (a) or (b), for the filing of any other document concerning an existing domestic limited liability company or a qualified foreign limited liability company that a person requests the administrator to complete on the same day as the day of the request, $200.00. The department may establish a deadline by which a person must submit a request for filing under this subdivision.
(e) For the filing of any formation or qualification document that a person requests the administrator to complete within 24 hours of the time the administrator receives the request, $50.00.
(f) For the filing of any other document concerning an existing domestic limited liability company or a qualified foreign limited liability company that a person requests the administrator to complete within 24 hours of the time the administrator receives the request, $100.00.

450.4105 Failure to promptly file document; notice of refusal to file; judicial review.

Sec. 105.

(1) If the administrator fails promptly to file a document submitted for filing under this act, the administrator, within 10 days after receipt from the person submitting the document for filing of a written request for the filing of the document, shall give to that person written notice of the refusal to file that states the reasons for the failure to file the document. If the document was originally submitted by electronic transmission, the administrator may give the written notice by electronic transmission.
(2) A person may seek judicial review of the administrator's decision under sections 103, 104, and 106 of the administrative

procedures act of 1969, 1969 PA 306, MCL 24.303, 24.304, and 24.305.

(3) If the administrator refuses or revokes the authorization of a foreign limited liability company to transact business in this state pursuant to this act, the foreign limited liability company may seek judicial review under sections 103, 104, and 106 of the administrative procedures act of 1969, 1969 PA 306, MCL 24.303, 24.304, and 24.305.

450.4106 Documents; inaccurate record or defective execution; certificate of correction; filing; signature; contents; effective date of corrected document.

Sec. 106.

(1) If a document relating to a domestic or foreign limited liability company filed with the administrator under this act was at the time of filing an inaccurate record of the action referred to in the document, or was defectively or erroneously executed, or was electronically transmitted and the electronic transmission was defective, the document may be corrected by filing with the administrator a certificate of correction on behalf of the company.
(2) The certificate shall be signed as provided by this act in the same manner as required for the document being corrected.
(3) The certificate shall set forth the name of the company, the date the document to be corrected was filed by the administrator, the provision in the document as it should have originally appeared, and if the execution was defective, the proper execution.
(4) The corrected document is effective in its corrected form as of its original filing date except as to a person who relied upon the inaccurate portion of the document and was as a result of the inaccurate portion of the document adversely affected by the correction.

Article 2

450.4201 Limited liability company; purpose.

Sec. 201.

A limited liability company may be formed under this act for any lawful purpose for which a domestic corporation or a domestic partnership could be formed, except as otherwise provided by law. A limited liability company formed to provide services in a learned profession, or more than 1 learned profession, shall comply with article 9.

450.4202 Limited liability company; formation; filing as evidence that all conditions performed; exception; duration.

Sec. 202.

(1) One or more persons, who may or may not become members, may be the organizers of a limited liability company by filing executed articles of organization.
(2) The existence of the limited liability company begins on the effective date of the articles of organization as provided in section 104. Filing is conclusive evidence that all conditions precedent required to be performed under this act are fulfilled and that the company is formed under this act, except in an action or special proceeding by the attorney general. The maximum duration of the limited liability company is perpetual unless otherwise provided in the articles of organization.

450.4203 Articles of organization; contents.

Sec. 203.

(1) The articles of organization shall contain all of the following:
    (a) The name of the limited liability company.
    (b) The purposes for which the limited liability company is formed. It is sufficient to state substantially, alone or with specifically enumerated purposes, that the limited liability company may engage in any activity for which limited liability companies may be formed under this act.
    (c) The street address, and the mailing address if different from the street address, of the limited liability company's initial registered office and the name of its initial resident agent at that address.
    (d) If the business of the limited liability company is to be managed by managers, a statement that the business is to be managed by or under the authority of managers.
    (e) The maximum duration of the limited liability company, if other than perpetual.
(2) The articles of organization may contain any provision not inconsistent with this act or another statute of this state, including any provision that is required or permitted to be in an operating agreement under this act.
(3) The articles of organization need not set out the powers of the limited liability company as described in section 210.

450.4204 Limited liability company; low-profit limited liability company; name; requirements; rights.

Sec. 204.

(1) Except as provided in subsection (2), the name of a domestic limited liability company shall contain the words "limited liability company", or the abbreviation "L.L.C." or "L.C.", with or without periods or other punctuation.
(2) The name of a low-profit limited liability company shall contain the words "low-profit limited liability company", or the abbreviation "L.3.C." or "l.3.c.", with or without periods or other punctuation.
(3) The name of a domestic or foreign limited liability company formed under or subject to this act shall conform to all of the following:
    (a) Shall not contain a word or phrase, or abbreviation or derivative of a word or phrase, that indicates or implies that the company is formed for a purpose other than the purpose or purposes permitted by its articles of organization.
    (b) Shall not contain the word "corporation" or "incorporated" or the abbreviation "corp." or "inc.".
    (c) Shall distinguish the name in the records in the office of the administrator from all of the following:
        (i) The name of a domestic limited liability company, or a foreign limited liability company authorized to transact business in this state, that is in good standing.
        (ii) The name of a corporation subject to the business corporation act, 1972 PA 284, MCL 450.1101 to 450.2098, or a nonprofit corporation subject to the nonprofit corporation act, 1982 PA 162, MCL 450.2101 to 450.3192.
        (iii) A name reserved, registered, or assumed under this act, under the business corporation act, 1972 PA 284, MCL 450.1101 to 450.2098, or under the nonprofit corporation act, 1982 PA 162, MCL 450.2101 to 450.3192.
        (iv) The name of a domestic or foreign limited partnership as filed or registered, reserved, or assumed under the Michigan revised uniform limited partnership act, 1982 PA 213, MCL 449.1101 to 449.2108.
    (d) Shall not contain a word or phrase, an abbreviation, or derivative of a word or phrase, the use of which is prohibited or restricted by any other statute of this state.
(4) If a foreign limited liability company is unable to obtain a certificate of authority to transact business in this state because

its name does not comply with subsections (1), (2), and (3), the foreign limited liability company may apply for authority to transact business in this state by adding to its name in the application a word, abbreviation, or other distinctive and distinguishing element, or alternatively, adopting for use in this state an assumed name otherwise available for use. If in the judgment of the administrator that name would comply with subsections (1), (2), and (3), those subsections do not bar the issuance to the foreign limited liability company of a certificate of authority to transact business in this state. The certificate of authority to transact business in this state issued to the foreign limited liability company shall be issued in the name applied for and the foreign limited liability company shall use that name in all its dealings with the administrator and in the transaction of business in this state.

(5) The fact that a limited liability company name complies with this section does not create substantive rights to the use of the name.

450.4204a Limited liability company licensed as nursing home; use of terms.

Sec. 204a.

A limited liability company formed or existing under or subject to this act that is licensed or is to be licensed as a nursing home under article 17 of the public health code, 1978 PA 368, MCL 333.20101 to 333.22260, may use the term "health center" or "health care center" or a term conveying a meaning substantially similar to those terms, or the term "rehabilitation center", as long as those terms do not conflict with the terms prohibited by section 21712 of the public health code, 1978 PA 368, MCL 333.21712.

450.4205 Reserving right to use of name; application; transfer of right.

Sec. 205.

(1) A person may reserve the right to use of a limited liability company name by executing and filing with the administrator an application to reserve the name. If the administrator finds that the name is available for use, the administrator shall reserve it for exclusive use of the applicant for a period expiring at the end of the sixth full calendar month following the month in which the application was filed.
(2) The right to exclusive use of a reserved name may be transferred to another person by filing a notice of the transfer, executed by the applicant for whom the name was reserved, and stating the name and address of the transferee.

450.4206 Transacting business under assumed name; certificate; effective period; extension; notice of expiration; rights not created; same name assumed in partnership or joint venture; transfer of assumed name to survivor; use of name by surviving company; assumed name of converted company; certificate of conversion.

Sec. 206.

(1) A domestic or foreign limited liability company may transact business under an assumed name or names other than its name as set forth in its articles of organization or certificate of authority, if not precluded from use of the assumed name or names under section 204(3), by filing a certificate stating the true name of the company and the assumed name or names under which business is to be transacted.

(2) A certificate of assumed name is effective, unless terminated by filing a certificate of termination or by the dissolution or withdrawal of the company, for a period expiring on December 31 of the fifth full calendar year following the year in which the certificate of assumed name was filed. The certificate of assumed name may be extended for additional consecutive periods of 5 full calendar years each by filing a similar certificate of assumed name not earlier than 90 days before the expiration of the initial or any subsequent 5-year period.

(3) The administrator shall notify a domestic or foreign limited liability company of the impending expiration of a certificate of assumed name not later than 90 days before the expiration of the initial or any subsequent 5-year period described in subsection (2).

(4) Filing a certificate of assumed name under this section does not create substantive rights to the use of a particular assumed name.

(5) The same name may be assumed by 2 or more limited liability companies or by 1 or more limited liability companies and 1 or more corporations, limited partnerships, or other enterprises participating together in a partnership or joint venture. Each participating limited liability company shall file a certificate of assumed name under this section.

(6) A limited liability company participating in a merger, or any other entity participating in a merger under section 705a, may transfer to the survivor the use of an assumed name for which a certificate of assumed name is on file with the administrator before the merger, if the transfer of the assumed name is noted in the certificate of merger as provided in section 703(1)(c), 705a(7)(c), or other applicable statute. The use of an assumed name transferred under this subsection may continue for the remaining effective period of the certificate of assumed name on file before the merger and the survivor may terminate or extend the certificate in accordance with subsection (2).

(7) A limited liability company surviving a merger may use as an assumed name the name of a merging limited liability company, or the name of any other entity participating in the merger under section 705a, by filing a certificate of assumed name under subsection (1) or by providing for the use of the assumed name in the certificate of merger. The surviving limited liability company may also file a certificate of assumed name under subsection (1) or provide in the certificate of merger for the use of an assumed name of a merging entity not transferred pursuant to subsection (6). A provision in the certificate of merger pursuant to this subsection is treated as a new certificate of assumed name.

(8) A business organization into which a domestic limited liability company has converted under section 708 may use an assumed name of the converting company, if the company has a certificate of assumed name for that assumed name on file with the administrator before the conversion, by providing for the use of the name as an assumed name in the certificate of conversion. The use of an assumed name under this subsection may continue for the remaining effective period of the certificate of assumed name on file before the conversion, and the surviving business organization may terminate or extend the certificate of assumed name in the manner described in subsection (2).

(9) A domestic limited liability company into which a business organization has converted under section 709 may use as an assumed name the name of the business organization converting into that company, or use as an assumed name an assumed name of that business organization, by filing a certificate of assumed name under subsection (2) or by providing for the use of that name or assumed name as an assumed name of the company in the certificate of conversion. A provision in the certificate of conversion under this subsection shall be treated as a new certificate of assumed name.

450.4207 Maintaining registered office and resident agent; service of process, notice, or demand; appointment of agent; annual statement; service of process by mail.

Sec. 207.

(1) Each domestic limited liability company and foreign limited liability company authorized to transact business in this state shall have and continuously maintain in this state both of the following:
    (a) A registered office that may, but need not be, the same as its place of business.
    (b) A resident agent. The resident agent may be either an individual resident in this state whose business office or residence is identical with the registered office or any of

the following having a business office identical with the registered office:
- (i) A domestic corporation.
- (ii) A foreign corporation authorized to transact business in this state.
- (iii) A domestic limited liability company.
- (iv) A foreign limited liability company authorized to transact business in this state.

(2) The resident agent appointed by a limited liability company is an agent of the company upon whom any process, notice, or demand required or permitted by law to be served upon the company may be served.

(3) A domestic limited liability company or foreign limited liability company authorized to transact business in this state shall file with the administrator an annual statement executed as provided in section 103 containing the name of its resident agent and the address of its registered office in this state. The statement shall be filed not later than February 15 of each year, except that a limited liability company formed after September 30 or a foreign limited liability company authorized to transact business in this state after September 30 need not file a statement on the February 15 immediately succeeding its formation or authorization.

(4) If a limited liability company fails to appoint or maintain an agent for service of process, or the agent for service of process cannot be found or served through the exercise of reasonable diligence, service of process may be made by delivering or mailing by registered mail to the administrator a summons and copy of the complaint.

450.4207a Certificate of good standing.

Sec. 207a.

(1) Except as provided in this section, and section 909 for a professional limited liability company, from the effective date of the articles of organization as provided in section 104 until dissolution for a domestic limited liability company, or from the effective date of the certificate of authority to transact business in this state until withdrawal from this state for a foreign limited liability company, a limited liability company is entitled to issuance by the administrator, upon request, of a certificate of good standing. A certificate of good standing issued to a domestic limited liability company shall state that it has been validly organized as a domestic limited liability company, that it is validly in existence under the laws of this state, and that it has satisfied its annual filing obligations. A certificate of good standing issued to a foreign limited liability company shall state that it has been validly authorized to transact business in this state, that it holds

a valid certificate of authority to transact business in this state, and that it has satisfied its annual filing obligations.

(2) If a domestic limited liability company or a foreign limited liability company authorized to transact business in this state fails to file an annual statement required by section 207 for 2 consecutive years, the administrator shall notify the company of the consequences of the failure to file under subsection (3).

(3) If a limited liability company does not file all annual statements it has failed to file, and the applicable fees, within 60 days after the administrator's notice under subsection (2) is sent, the limited liability company is not in good standing. A limited liability company that is not in good standing is not entitled to issuance by the administrator of a certificate of good standing described in subsection (1), the name of the company is available for use by another entity filing with the administrator, and the administrator shall not accept for filing any document submitted by the limited liability company other than a certificate of restoration of good standing provided for in subsection (4). A limited liability company that is not in good standing remains in existence and may continue to transact business in this state.

(4) A domestic limited liability company or a foreign limited liability company authorized to transact business in this state that is not in good standing under subsection (3) may file a certificate of restoration of good standing, accompanied by the annual statements and fees for all of the years for which they were not filed and paid, and the fee for filing the certificate of restoration of good standing. The certificate shall include all of the following:

    (a) The name of the limited liability company at the time it ceased to be in good standing. If that name is not available when the certificate of restoration of good standing is filed, the limited liability company shall select a new name that complies with section 204. The new name shall be the name of the domestic limited liability company or the name used in this state by the foreign limited liability company from the date of filing of the certificate.

    (b) The name of the limited liability company's current resident agent and the address of the current registered office in this state.

    (c) A statement that the certificate is accompanied by the annual statements and applicable fees for all of the years for which statements were not filed and fees were not paid.

450.4208 Resident agent; resignation; notice; appointment of successor; termination of appointment.

Sec. 208.

(1) A resident agent of a limited liability company may resign as agent upon filing a written notice of resignation with the administrator and with a member or manager of the limited liability company.
(2) The company shall promptly appoint a successor resident agent.
(3) The appointment of the resigning agent terminates 30 days after the date the notice is filed with the administrator or upon the appointment of a successor, whichever occurs first.

450.4209 Changing registered office or resident agent; statement; filing; contents; changing business or residence address of resident agent.

Sec. 209.

(1) A domestic limited liability company or foreign limited liability company authorized to transact business in this state may change its registered office or resident agent, or both, upon filing with the administrator a statement executed as provided in section 103 and setting forth all of the following:
    (a) The name of the limited liability company.
    (b) The address of its then registered office and the new address if the registered office is to be changed.
    (c) The name of its then resident agent and the name of the successor if the resident agent is to be changed.
    (d) A statement that the address of the registered office and the address of the resident agent are identical.
    (e) A statement that the change was authorized in accordance with an operating agreement, or, if not provided for in an operating agreement, by affirmative vote of a majority of the members voting in accordance with section 502(1) or managers voting in accordance with section 405.
(2) If a resident agent changes its business or residence address to another place within this state, the resident agent may change the address of the registered office of the domestic or foreign limited liability company of which the person is a resident agent by filing a statement as required in subsection (1) and mailing a copy of the statement to the limited liability company. The statement need only to be signed by the resident agent and need not contain the statement required by subsection (1)(e).

450.4210 Limited liability company; powers.

Sec. 210.

Subject to the limitations provided in this act, any other statute of this state, or its articles of organization, a limited liability company has all powers necessary or convenient to effect any purpose for which the company is formed, including all powers granted to corporations in the business corporation act, 1972 PA 284, MCL 450.1101 to 450.2098.

450.4211 Validity of action or transfer of property; asserting lack of capacity or power.

Sec. 211.

An act of a limited liability company and a transfer of real or personal property to or by a limited liability company, otherwise lawful, is not invalid because the company was without capacity or power to do the act or make or receive the transfer, except that the lack of capacity or power may be asserted in any of the following:
(a) In an action by a member against the company to enjoin the doing of an act or the transfer of real or personal property by or to the company.
(b) In an action by or in the right of the company to procure a judgment in its favor against an incumbent or former member or manager of the company for loss or damage due to an unauthorized act of that member or manager.
(c) In an action or special proceeding by the attorney general to dissolve the company or to enjoin it from the transaction of unauthorized business.

450.4212 Interest rate; agreement.

Sec. 212.

A domestic or foreign limited liability company, whether or not formed at the request of a lender, may agree in writing to pay any rate of interest as long as that rate of interest is not in excess of the rate set forth in Act No. 259 of the Public Acts of 1968, being sections 438.41 to 438.42 of the Michigan Compiled Laws.

450.4213 Registered office or principal place of business; documents required to be kept.

Sec. 213.

A limited liability company shall keep at its registered office or principal place of business in this state all of the following:
(a) A current list of the full name and last known address of each member and manager.
(b) A copy of the articles or restated articles of organization, together with any amendments to the articles.
(c) Copies of the limited liability company's federal, state, and local tax returns and reports, if any, for the 3 most recent years.
(d) Copies of any financial statements of the limited liability company for the 3 most recent years.
(e) Copies of operating agreements.
(f) Copies of records that would enable a member to determine the members' relative shares of the limited liability company's distributions and the members' relative voting rights.

450.4214 Conflict between articles of organization and operating agreement.

Sec. 214.

If there is a conflict between the articles of organization and an operating agreement of a limited liability company, the articles of organization shall control.

450.4215 Operating agreement unenforceable.

Sec. 215.

An operating agreement of a limited liability company that has 1 member is not unenforceable because only 1 person is a party to the operating agreement.

450.4216 Limited liability company; powers.

Sec. 216.

Except as otherwise provided in an operating agreement, a limited liability company may do any of the following:

(a) Indemnify, hold harmless, and defend a member, manager, or other person from and against any and all losses, expenses, claims, and demands sustained by that person, except that the

company may not indemnify a person for conduct described in section 407(a), (b), or (c).
(b) Purchase and maintain insurance on behalf of a member, manager, or other person against any liability or expense asserted against or incurred by that person, whether or not the company may indemnify that person under subdivision (a).

Article 3

450.4301 Members; contribution.

Sec. 301.

(1) A contribution of a member to a limited liability company may consist of any tangible or intangible property or benefit to the company, including cash, property, services performed, promissory notes, contracts for services to be performed, or other binding obligation to contribute cash or property or to perform services.
(2) A contribution of an obligation to contribute cash or property or to perform services may be in exchange for a present membership interest or for a future membership interest, including a future profits interest, as provided in an operating agreement.

450.4302 Promise by member to contribute; enforcement; obligation to perform; rights of company; compromising obligation; enforcement by creditor of original member's obligation.

Sec. 302.

(1) A promise by a member to contribute to the limited liability company is not enforceable unless the promise is in writing and signed by the member.
(2) Unless otherwise provided in an operating agreement, a member is obligated to the limited liability company to perform any enforceable promise to contribute cash or property or to perform services, even if the member is unable to perform because of death, disability, or other reason. If a member does not make the required contribution of property or services, the member is obligated, at the option of the limited liability company, to contribute cash equal to that portion of value of the stated contribution that is not made.
(3) The rights of the limited liability company under subsection (2) are in addition to any other rights that the limited liability company may have under an operating agreement or applicable law.

(4) Unless otherwise provided in an operating agreement, a member's obligation to make a contribution or to return money or other property paid or distributed in violation of this act may be compromised only upon the unanimous vote of the members of the limited liability company entitled to vote. Notwithstanding a compromise of a member's obligation, a creditor of a limited liability company who extends credit or otherwise acts in reliance on the member's obligation after the member signs a writing that reflects the obligation and before the amendment of the writing to reflect the compromise may enforce the member's original obligation.

450.4303 Distribution of assets; allocation; manner; basis.

Sec. 303.

(1) Distributions of cash or other assets of a limited liability company shall be allocated among the members and among classes of members in the manner provided in an operating agreement. If an operating agreement does not provide for an allocation, distributions shall be allocated as follows:
    (a) Prior to July 1, 1997, on the basis of the value, as stated in the records the limited liability company is required to keep under section 213 or as determined by any other reasonable method, of the contributions made by each member to the extent that the contributions have been received by the limited liability company and have not been returned.
    (b) On and after July 1, 1997, except as otherwise provided in subsection (2), in equal shares to all members. A membership interest held by 2 or more persons, whether as fiduciaries, members of a partnership, tenants in common, joint tenants, tenants by the entirety, or otherwise, is considered as held by 1 member for an allocation under this subdivision.
(2) If a limited liability company in existence before July 1, 1997 allocated distributions on the basis of subsection (1)(a), the limited liability company shall continue to allocate distributions pursuant to subsection (1)(a) until the allocation is changed by an operating agreement.

450.4304 Distribution; conditions for receiving.

Sec. 304.

(1) Except as otherwise provided in this act and subject to subsection (2), a member is entitled to receive a distribution from a limited liability company before the withdrawal of the member

from the limited liability company or before the dissolution and winding up of the limited liability company to the extent and at the times or upon the happening of the events specified in an operating agreement.

(2) If an operating agreement does not address a member's right to receive a distribution before the withdrawal of the member from the limited liability company or before the dissolution and winding up of the limited liability company, the unanimous approval of the members is required for any distribution to that member.

450.4305 Distributions to withdrawing member.

Sec. 305.

Until the effective date of withdrawal, a withdrawing member shall share in any distribution made in accordance with section 304. An operating agreement may provide for an additional distribution to a withdrawing member. If a provision in an operating agreement permits withdrawal but is silent on an additional withdrawal distribution, a member withdrawing in accordance with the operating agreement is entitled to receive as a distribution, within a reasonable time after withdrawal, the fair value of the member's interest in the limited liability company as of the date of withdrawal based upon the member's share of distributions as determined under section 303.

450.4306 Distributions; demand, acceptance, and receipt of distribution; form.

Sec. 306.

Except as provided in an operating agreement, a member, regardless of the nature of the member's contribution, has no right to demand and receive a distribution from a limited liability company in any form other than cash, and a member may not be compelled to accept from a limited liability company a distribution of an asset in kind to the extent that the percentage of the asset distributed to the member exceeds a percentage of that asset that is equal to the percentage in which the member shares in distributions from the limited liability company.

450.4307 Distributions prohibited under certain situations; exceptions; effect of distribution under subsection (1); remedies available; future

payments to withdrawing members; effect of subsection (1) on third party; asserting legal or equitable rights.

Sec. 307.

(1) Except as otherwise provided in subsection (5), a distribution shall not be made if, after giving the distribution effect, 1 or more of the following situations would occur:
    (a) The limited liability company would not be able to pay its debts as they become due in the usual course of business.
    (b) The limited liability company's total assets would be less than the sum of its total liabilities plus, unless an operating agreement provides otherwise, the amount that would be needed, if the limited liability company were to be dissolved at the time of the distribution, to satisfy the preferential rights of other members upon dissolution that are superior to the rights of the member or members receiving the distribution.

(2) The limited liability company may base a determination that a distribution is not prohibited under subsection (1) on financial statements prepared on the basis of accounting practices and principles that are reasonable under the circumstances, on a fair valuation, or on another method that is reasonable under the circumstances.

(3) The effect of a distribution under subsection (1) is measured at the following times:
    (a) Except as provided in subsection (5), in the case of a distribution to a withdrawing member, as of the earlier of the date money or other property is transferred or debt incurred by the limited liability company, or the date the member ceases to be a member.
    (b) In the case of any other distribution of indebtedness, as of the date the indebtedness is authorized if distribution occurs within 120 days after the date of authorization, or the date the indebtedness is distributed if it occurs more than 120 days after the date of authorization.
    (c) In all other cases, as of the date the distribution is authorized if the payment occurs within 120 days after the date of authorization, or the date the payment is made if it occurs more than 120 days after the date of authorization.

(4) At the time a member becomes entitled to receive a distribution, the member has the status of, and is entitled to all remedies available to, a creditor of the limited liability company with respect to the distribution. A company's indebtedness to a member incurred by reason of a distribution made in accordance with this section is at parity with the company's indebtedness to its general, unsecured creditors except as otherwise agreed.

(5) If the limited liability company distributes an obligation to make future payments to a withdrawing member, and distribution of the obligation would otherwise be prohibited under subsection (1) at the time it is made, the company may issue the obligation and the following apply:
    (a) The portion of the obligation that could have been distributed without violating subsection (1) is indebtedness to the withdrawing member under subsection (4).
    (b) All of the following apply to the portion of the obligation that exceeds the amount of the obligation that is indebtedness to the withdrawing member under subdivision (a):
        (i) At any time prior to the due date of the obligation, payments of principal and interest may be made as a distribution to the extent that a distribution may then be made under this section.
        (ii) At any time on or after the due date, the obligation to pay principal and interest is considered distributed and treated as indebtedness described in subsection (4) to the extent that a distribution may then be made under this section.
    (c) Unless otherwise provided in an agreement with the withdrawing member, the obligation is considered a liability or debt for purposes of determining whether distributions other than payments on the obligation may be made under this section, except for purposes of determining whether distributions may be made to members having preferential rights superior to the rights of the withdrawing member.

(6) The enforceability of a guaranty or other undertaking by a third party relating to a distribution is not affected by the prohibition of the distribution under subsection (1).

(7) If a claim is made to recover a distribution made contrary to subsection (1) or if a violation of subsection (1) is raised as a defense to a claim based upon a distribution, this section does not prevent the person receiving the distribution from asserting a right of rescission or other legal or equitable rights.

450.4308 Distribution; violating operating agreement or MCL 450.4307; liability of members or managers; presumption of assent; knowledge of violation; contribution; commencement of proceeding.

Sec. 308.

(1) A member or manager that votes for or assents to a distribution in violation of an operating agreement or section 307 is personally liable, jointly and severally, to the limited liability company for the amount of the distribution that exceeds what could have been distributed without violating the operating agreement or section 307 if it is established that the member or manager did not comply with section 404.

(2) For purposes of liability under subsection (1), a member or manager entitled to participate in a decision to make a distribution is presumed to have assented to a distribution unless the member or manager does 1 of the following:
    (a) Votes against the distribution.
    (b) Files a written dissent with the limited liability company within a reasonable time after the member or manager has knowledge of the decision.

(3) A member that accepts or receives a distribution with knowledge of facts indicating it is in violation of an operating agreement or section 307 is liable to the limited liability company for the amount the member accepts or receives that exceeds the member's share of the amount that could have been distributed without violating section 307 or the operating agreement.

(4) Each member or manager held liable under subsection (1) for an unlawful distribution is entitled to contribution from each other member or manager who could be held liable under subsection (1) or (3). The contribution of a person held liable under both subsections (1) and (3) shall not exceed the person's liability under either subsection (1) or (3), whichever is greater.

(5) A proceeding under this section is barred unless it is commenced within 2 years after the date on which the effect of the distribution is measured under section 307.

Article 4

450.4401 Management vested in members.

Sec. 401.

Unless the articles of organization state that the business of the limited liability company is to be managed by 1 or more managers, the business of the limited liability company shall be managed by the members, subject to any provision in an operating agreement

restricting or enlarging the management rights and duties of any member or group of members. If management is vested in the members, both of the following apply:
(a) The members are considered managers for purposes of applying this act, including section 406 regarding the agency authority of managers, unless the context clearly requires otherwise.
(b) The members have, and are subject to, all duties and liabilities of managers and to all limitations on liability and indemnification rights of managers.

450.4402 Managers; delegation; qualifications; number; notice of delegation.

Sec. 402.

(1) The articles of organization may provide that the business of the limited liability company shall be managed by or under the authority of 1 or more managers. The delegation of the management of a limited liability company to managers is subject to any provision in the articles of organization or in an operating agreement restricting or enlarging the management rights and duties of any manager or group of managers.
(2) An operating agreement may prescribe qualifications for managers, including a requirement that the managers be members.
(3) The number of managers shall be specified in or fixed in accordance with an operating agreement.
(4) If the articles of organization delegate management of a limited liability company to managers, the articles of organization constitute notice to third parties that managers, not members, have the agency authority described in section 406.

450.4403 Managers; selection; vote; removal; notice.

Sec. 403.

(1) A vote of a majority in interest of the members entitled to vote in accordance with section 502(1) is required to select 1 or more managers to fill initial positions or vacancies.
(2) The members may remove 1 or more managers with or without cause unless an operating agreement provides that managers may be removed only for cause.
(3) The members may remove a manager for cause only at a meeting called expressly for that purpose, and the manager shall have reasonable advance notice of the allegations against that manager and an opportunity to be heard at the meeting.

450.4404 Managers; duties; action for failure to perform duties.

Sec. 404.

(1) A manager shall discharge the duties of manager in good faith, with the care an ordinarily prudent person in a like position would exercise under similar circumstances, and in a manner the manager reasonably believes to be in the best interests of the limited liability company.

(2) In discharging the manager's duties, a manager may rely on information, opinions, reports, or statements, including, but not limited to, financial statements or other financial data, if prepared or presented by any of the following:

    (a) One or more other managers or members or employees of the limited liability company whom the manager reasonably believes to be reliable and competent in the matter presented.

    (b) Legal counsel, public accountants, engineers, or other persons as to matters the manager reasonably believes are within the person's professional or expert competence.

    (c) A committee of managers of which the manager is not a member if the manager reasonably believes the committee merits confidence.

(3) A manager is not entitled to rely on the information, opinions, reports, or statements described in subsection (2) if the manager has knowledge concerning the matter in question that makes reliance otherwise permitted by subsection (2) unwarranted.

(4) A manager is not liable for an action taken as a manager or the failure to take an action if the manager performs the duties of the manager's office in compliance with this section.

(5) Except as otherwise provided in an operating agreement or by vote of the members pursuant to section 502(4) and (7), a manager shall account to the limited liability company and hold as trustee for it any profit or benefit derived by the manager from any transaction connected with the conduct or winding up of the limited liability company or from any personal use by the manager of its property.

(6) An action against a manager for failure to perform the duties imposed by this act shall be commenced within 3 years after the cause of action has accrued or within 2 years after the cause of action is discovered or should reasonably have been discovered by the complainant, whichever occurs first.

450.4405 Managers; voting requirements.

Sec. 405.

(1) Except as otherwise provided in the articles of organization or an operating agreement, voting by managers shall be as provided in this section.
(2) If management of a limited liability company is delegated to managers under section 402 and the limited liability company has more than 1 manager, each manager has 1 vote and the vote of a majority of all managers is required to decide or resolve any difference on any matter connected with carrying on the business of the limited liability company that is within the scope of the managers' authority.
(3) If management of a limited liability company remains in the members, section 502 applies to voting by the members.

450.4406 Manager as agent.

Sec. 406.

A manager is an agent of the limited liability company for the purpose of its business, and the act of a manager, including the execution in the limited liability company name of any instrument, that apparently carries on in the usual way the business of the limited liability company of which the manager is a manager binds the limited liability company, unless both of the following apply:
(a) The manager does not have the authority to act for the limited liability company in that particular matter.
(b) The person with whom the manager is dealing has actual knowledge that the manager lacks authority to act or the articles of organization or this act establishes that the manager lacks authority to act.

450.4407 Managers; eliminating or limiting liability; exceptions.

Sec. 407.

A provision in the articles of organization or an operating agreement may eliminate or limit the monetary liability of a manager to the limited liability company or its members for breach of any duty established in section 404, except that the provision does not eliminate or limit the liability of a manager for any of the following:
(a) The receipt of a financial benefit to which the manager is not entitled.
(b) Liability under section 308.
(c) A knowing violation of law.
(d) An act or omission occurring before the date when the provision becomes effective.

450.4409 Manager or agent with interest in company; effect; majority vote by members with no interest in transaction; claims.

Sec. 409.

(1) Except as otherwise provided in an operating agreement, a transaction in which a manager or agent of a limited liability company is determined to have an interest shall not, because of the interest, be enjoined, be set aside, or give rise to an award of damages or other sanctions, in a proceeding by a member or by or in the right of the company, if the manager or agent interested in the transaction establishes any of the following:
    (a) The transaction was fair to the company at the time entered into.
    (b) The material facts of the transaction and the manager's or agent's interest were disclosed or known to the managers and the managers authorized, approved, or ratified the transaction.
    (c) The material facts of the transaction and the manager's or agent's interest were disclosed or known to the members entitled to vote and they authorized, approved, or ratified the transaction.

(2) Except as otherwise provided in the articles of organization or an operating agreement, a transaction is authorized, approved, or ratified for purposes of subsection (1)(b) if it receives the affirmative vote of a majority of the managers that have no interest in the transaction. The presence of, or a vote cast by, a manager with an interest in the transaction does not affect the validity of an action taken under subsection (1)(b).

(3) Except as otherwise provided in the articles of organization or an operating agreement, a transaction is authorized, approved, or ratified for purposes of subsection (1)(c) if it receives a majority of votes cast by the members entitled to vote that do not have an interest in the transaction.

(4) Satisfying the requirements of subsection (1) does not preclude other claims relating to a transaction in which a manager or agent is determined to have an interest. Those claims shall be evaluated under principles of law applicable to a transaction in which a similarly situated person does not have an interest.

Article 5

450.4501 Members; admission; liability for acts, debts, or obligations.

Sec. 501.

(1) A person may be admitted as a member of a limited liability company in connection with the formation of the limited liability company in any of the following ways:
    (a) If an operating agreement includes requirements for admission, by complying with those requirements.
    (b) If an operating agreement does not include requirements for admission, if either of the following are met:
        (i) The person signs the initial operating agreement.
        (ii) The person's status as a member is reflected in the records, tax filings, or other written statements of the limited liability company.
    (c) In any manner established in a written agreement of the members.
(2) A person may be admitted as a member of a limited liability company after the formation of the limited liability company in any of the following ways:
    (a) If the person is acquiring a membership interest directly from the limited liability company, by complying with the provisions of an operating agreement prescribing the requirements for admission or, in the absence of provisions prescribing the requirements for admission in an operating agreement, upon the unanimous vote of the members entitled to vote.
    (b) If the person is an assignee of a membership interest, as provided in section 506.
    (c) If the person is becoming a member of a surviving limited liability company as the result of a merger or conversion approved under this act, as provided in the plan of merger or plan of conversion.
(3) A limited liability company may admit a person as a member that does not make a contribution or incur an obligation to make a contribution to the limited liability company.
(4) Unless otherwise provided by law or in an operating agreement, a person that is a member or manager, or both, of a limited liability company is not liable for the acts, debts, or obligations of the limited liability company.

450.4502 Members; voting rights.

Sec. 502.

(1) An operating agreement may establish and allocate the voting rights of members and may provide that certain members or groups of members have only limited or no voting rights. If an operating agreement does not address voting rights, votes are allocated as follows:
- (a) Before July 1, 1997, the members of a limited liability company shall vote in proportion to their shares of distributions of the company, as determined under section 303.
- (b) On and after July 1, 1997, except as otherwise provided in subsection (2), each member of a limited liability company has 1 vote. For purposes of this subdivision, a membership interest held by 2 or more persons, whether as fiduciaries, members of a partnership, tenants in common, joint tenants, tenants by the entirety, or otherwise, is considered held by 1 member.

(2) If a limited liability company in existence before July 1, 1997 allocated votes on the basis of subsection (1)(a), the company shall continue to allocate votes pursuant to subsection (1)(a) until the allocation is changed by an operating agreement.

(3) If a membership interest that has voting rights is held by 2 or more persons, whether as fiduciaries, members of a partnership, tenants in common, joint tenants, tenants by the entirety, or otherwise, the voting of the interest shall be in accordance with the instrument or order appointing them or creating the relationship if a copy of that instrument or order is furnished to the limited liability company. If an instrument or order is not furnished to the limited liability company, 1 of the following applies to the voting of that membership interest:
- (a) If an operating agreement applies to the voting of the membership interest, the vote shall be in accordance with that operating agreement.
- (b) If an operating agreement does not apply to the voting of the membership interest and only 1 of the persons that hold the membership interest votes, that person's vote determines the voting of the membership interest.
- (c) If an operating agreement does not apply to the voting of the membership interest and 2 or more of the persons that hold the membership interest vote, the vote of a majority determines the voting of the membership interest, and if there is no majority, the voting of the membership interest is divided among those voting.

(4) Only members of a limited liability company, and not its managers, may authorize the following actions:
- (a) The dissolution of the limited liability company under section 801(c).

(b) Merger of the limited liability company under sections 701 through 706.
(c) An amendment to the articles of organization.
(d) Conversion of the limited liability company under section 708.

(5) Except as otherwise provided in the articles of organization or an operating agreement, members have the voting rights provided in section 409 regarding transactions in which a manager or agent has an interest.

(6) Unless otherwise provided in an operating agreement, the sale, exchange, lease, or other transfer of all or substantially all of the assets of a limited liability company, other than in the ordinary course of business, may be authorized only by a vote of the members entitled to vote.

(7) The articles of organization or an operating agreement may provide for additional voting rights of members of the limited liability company.

(8) Unless the vote of a greater percentage of the voting interest of members is required by this act, the articles of organization, or an operating agreement, a vote of a majority in interest of the members entitled to vote is required to approve any matter submitted for a vote of the members.

450.4503 Members; obtaining certain financial statements and tax returns; inspecting and copying records; obtaining other information; formal accounting of company's affairs.

Sec. 503.

(1) Upon written request of a member, a limited liability company shall send a copy of its most recent annual financial statement and its most recent federal, state, and local income tax returns, and any other returns or filings the limited liability company has submitted or is required to submit to any federal, state, local, or other governmental taxing authority, to the member by mail or electronic transmission.

(2) Upon reasonable request, a member may obtain true and full information regarding the current state of a limited liability company's financial condition.

(3) Upon reasonable written request and during ordinary business hours, a member or the member's designated representative may inspect and copy, at the member's expense, any of the records a limited liability company is required to maintain under section 213, at the location where the records are kept.

(4) Upon reasonable written request, a member may obtain other information regarding a limited liability company's affairs or may inspect, personally or through a representative and during

ordinary business hours, other books and records of the limited liability company, as is just and reasonable.

(5) A member may have a formal accounting of a limited liability company's affairs, as provided in an operating agreement or whenever circumstances render it just and reasonable.

450.4504 Membership interest as personal property.

Sec. 504.

(1) A membership interest is personal property and may be held in any manner in which personal property may be held. A husband and wife may hold a membership interest in joint tenancy in the same manner and subject to the same restrictions, consequences, and conditions that apply to the ownership of real estate held jointly by a husband and wife under the laws of this state, with full right of ownership by survivorship in case of the death of either.

(2) A member has no interest in specific limited liability company property.

450.4505 Membership interest; assignment; liability of assignee; assignor as member; liability of assignor not released.

Sec. 505.

(1) Except as provided in an operating agreement, a membership interest is assignable in whole or in part.

(2) An assignment of a membership interest does not of itself entitle the assignee to participate in the management and affairs of a limited liability company or to become or exercise any rights of a member. An assignment entitles the assignee to receive, to the extent assigned, only the distributions to which the assignor would be entitled.

(3) Unless otherwise provided in an operating agreement and except to the extent assumed by agreement, an assignee has no liability as a member solely as a result of the assignment.

(4) Except as provided in an operating agreement, a member ceases to be a member when the member's entire membership interest is assigned. The assignor is not released from any liability to the company under sections 302 and 308 even if the assignee becomes a member.

450.4506 Assignee of membership interest; conditions for membership; rights and powers; liability for obligations of assignor.

Sec. 506.

(1) Unless otherwise provided in an operating agreement, an assignee of a membership interest in a limited liability company that has more than 1 member may become a member only upon a unanimous vote of the members entitled to vote. An assignee of a membership interest in a limited liability company that has 1 member may become a member in accordance with the terms of the agreement between the member and the assignee.

(2) An assignee that becomes a member of a limited liability company has, to the extent assigned, the rights and powers, and is subject to the restrictions and liabilities, of a member under the articles of organization, an operating agreement, and this act. An assignee that becomes a member also is liable for any obligations the assignor has to make contributions and to return distributions under sections 302 and 308(3). An assignee is not obligated for liabilities unknown to the assignee at the time the assignee became a member unless the liabilities are shown on the financial records of the limited liability company.

450.4507 Charging membership interest with payment of judgment; rights of judgment creditor; rights and powers of member; charging order as lien on membership interest; section as exclusive remedy.

Sec. 507.

(1) If a court of competent jurisdiction receives an application from any judgment creditor of a member of a limited liability company, the court may charge the membership interest of the member with payment of the unsatisfied amount of judgment with interest.

(2) If a limited liability company is served with a charging order and notified of the terms of that order, then to the extent described in the order, the member's judgment creditor described in the order is entitled to receive only any distribution or distributions to which the judgment creditor is entitled with respect to the member's membership interest.

(3) This act does not deprive any member of the benefit of any exemption laws applicable to the member's membership interest.

(4) Unless otherwise provided in an operating agreement or admitted as a member under section 501, a judgment creditor of a member that obtains a charging order does not become a member of the limited liability company, and the member that is the subject of the charging order remains a member of the limited liability

company and retains all rights and powers of membership except the right to receive distributions to the extent charged.
(5) A charging order is a lien on the membership interest of the member that is the subject of the charging order. However, a person may not foreclose on that lien or on the membership interest under this act or any other law, and the charging order is not an assignment of the member's membership interest for purposes of section 505(4).
(6) This section provides the exclusive remedy by which a judgment creditor of a member may satisfy a judgment out of the member's membership interest in a limited liability company. A court order to which a member may have been entitled that requires a limited liability company to take an action, provide an accounting, or answer an inquiry is not available to a judgment creditor of that member attempting to satisfy a judgment out of the member's membership interest, and a court may not issue an order to a judgment creditor.

450.4508 Encumbrance against membership interest; effect.

Sec. 508.

Unless otherwise provided in an operating agreement, the pledge or granting of a security interest, lien, or other encumbrance in or against any or all of the membership interest of a member does not cause the member to cease to be a member or to lose the power to exercise any rights or powers of a member.

450.4509 Withdrawal of member; distribution; expulsion.

Sec. 509.

(1) A member may withdraw from a limited liability company only as provided in an operating agreement. A member withdrawing pursuant to an operating agreement may become entitled to a withdrawal distribution as described in section 305.
(2) An operating agreement may provide for the expulsion of a member or for other events the occurrence of which will result in a person ceasing to be a member of the limited liability company.

450.4510 Commencement and maintenance of civil suit by company; conditions.

Sec. 510.

A member may commence and maintain a civil suit in the right of a limited liability company if all of the following conditions are met:

(a) Either management of the limited liability company is vested in a manager or managers that have the sole authority to cause the limited liability company to sue in its own right or management of the limited liability company is reserved to the members but the plaintiff does not have the authority to cause the limited liability company to sue in its own right under the provisions of an operating agreement.
(b) The plaintiff has made written demand on the managers or the members with the authority requesting that the managers or members cause the limited liability company to take suitable action.
(c) Ninety days have expired from the date the demand was made unless the member has earlier been notified that the demand has been rejected or unless irreparable injury to the limited liability company would result by waiting for the expiration of the 90-day period.
(d) The plaintiff was a member of the limited liability company at the time of the act or omission of which the member complains, or the member's status as a member devolved upon the member by operation of law or pursuant to this act or the terms of an operating agreement from a person that was a member at that time.
(e) The plaintiff fairly and adequately represents the interests of the limited liability company in enforcing the right of the limited liability company.
(f) The plaintiff continues to be a member until the time of judgment, unless the failure to continue to be a member is the result of action by the limited liability company in which the former member did not acquiesce and the demand was made before the termination of the former member's status as a member.

450.4511 Investigation of allegations; stay of derivative proceeding.

Sec. 511.

If the limited liability company commences an investigation of the allegations made in the demand or complaint, the court may stay any derivative proceeding for a period as the court considers appropriate.

450.4512 Dismissal of derivative proceeding; findings; burden of proof; determination; "disinterested" defined.

Sec. 512.

(1) The court shall dismiss a derivative proceeding if, on motion by the limited liability company, the court finds that 1 of the groups specified in subsection (3) has made a determination in good faith after conducting a reasonable investigation upon which its

conclusions are based that the maintenance of the derivative proceeding is not in the best interests of the company.
(2) If the determination is made pursuant to subsection (3)(a) or (b), the company has the burden of proving the good faith of the group making the determination and the reasonableness of the investigation. If the determination is made pursuant to subsection (3)(c), the plaintiff has the burden of proving that the determination was not made in good faith or that the investigation was not reasonable.
(3) A determination under subsection (1) may be made by any 1 of the following:
    (a) By a majority vote of the disinterested managers or members having the authority to cause the company to sue in its own right, if the disinterested managers or members constitute a majority of those having the authority to cause the company to sue in its own right.
    (b) By a majority vote of a committee consisting of 2 or more disinterested managers or members appointed by a majority vote of disinterested managers or members, whether or not the disinterested managers or members constitute a majority of those having the authority to cause the company to sue in its own right.
    (c) By a panel of 1 or more disinterested persons appointed by the court upon motion by the company.
(4) For purposes of this section, "disinterested" means a person who is not a party to a derivative proceeding or a person who is a party if the limited liability company demonstrates that the claim asserted against the person is frivolous or insubstantial.

450.4513 Discontinued or settled derivative proceeding; court approval required; notice; expense.

Sec. 513.

A derivative proceeding may not be discontinued or settled without the court's approval. If the court determines that a proposed discontinuance or settlement will substantially affect the interests of members of the limited liability company, the court shall direct that notice be given to the members affected. If notice is directed to be given to the affected members, the court may determine whether 1 or more of the parties to the action shall bear the expense of giving the notice, in the amount as the court determines and finds to be reasonable under the circumstances. The amount of expense shall be awarded as special costs of the action and is recoverable in the same manner as statutory taxable costs.

450.4514 Termination of derivative proceeding; court order.

Sec. 514.

If a derivative proceeding is terminated, the court may order 1 of the following:

(a) The plaintiff to pay any of the defendants' reasonable expenses, including reasonable attorney fees, incurred in defending the proceeding if it finds that the proceeding was commenced or maintained in bad faith or without reasonable cause.
(b) The limited liability company to pay the plaintiff's reasonable expenses, including reasonable attorney fees, incurred in the proceeding if it finds that the proceeding has resulted in a substantial benefit to the company. The court shall direct the plaintiff to account to the company for any proceeds received by the plaintiff in excess of expenses awarded by the court, except that this provision does not apply to a judgment rendered for the benefit of an injured member only and limited to a recovery of the loss or damage sustained by that member.

450.4515 Action in circuit court; grounds; order or grant of relief; "willfully unfair and oppressive conduct" defined.

Sec. 515.

(1) A member of a limited liability company may bring an action in the circuit court of the county in which the limited liability company's principal place of business or registered office is located to establish that acts of the managers or members in control of the limited liability company are illegal or fraudulent or constitute willfully unfair and oppressive conduct toward the limited liability company or the member. If the member establishes grounds for relief, the circuit court may issue an order or grant relief as it considers appropriate, including, but not limited to, an order providing for any of the following:
    (a) The dissolution and liquidation of the assets and business of the limited liability company.
    (b) The cancellation or alteration of a provision in the articles of organization or in an operating agreement.
    (c) The direction, alteration, or prohibition of an act of the limited liability company or its members or managers.
    (d) The purchase at fair value of the member's interest in the limited liability company, either by the company or by any members responsible for the wrongful acts.
    (e) An award of damages to the limited liability company or to the member. An action seeking an award of damages must be commenced within 3 years after the cause of action under this section has accrued or within 2 years

after the member discovers or reasonably should have discovered the cause of action under this section, whichever occurs first.

(2) As used in this section, "willfully unfair and oppressive conduct" means a continuing course of conduct or a significant action or series of actions that substantially interferes with the interests of the member as a member. Willfully unfair and oppressive conduct may include the termination of employment or limitations on employment benefits to the extent that the actions interfere with distributions or other member interests disproportionately as to the affected member. The term does not include conduct or actions that are permitted by the articles of organization, an operating agreement, another agreement to which the member is a party, or a consistently applied written company policy or procedure.

Article 6

450.4601 Articles of organization; amendment.

Sec. 601.

A limited liability company may amend its articles of organization if the amendment contains only provisions that might lawfully be contained in original articles of organization filed at the time the amendment is made.

450.4602 Articles of organization; conditions requiring amendment.

Sec. 602.

A limited liability company shall amend its articles of organization if any of the following occur:
(a) A change in the name of the limited liability company.
(b) A change in the purposes of the limited liability company.
(c) A change to or from the management of the limited liability company by managers.
(d) A change in the maximum duration of the limited liability company.
(e) A statement in the articles of organization has become false or erroneous, except that a change in registered office or resident agent may be made as provided for in section 209.

450.4603 Articles of organization; certificate of amendment; filing; contents.

Sec. 603.

The articles of organization are amended by filing a certificate of amendment signed as provided in section 103 that contains all of the following:
(a) The name of the limited liability company.
(b) The date of filing of its original articles of organization.
(c) The entire article or articles being amended, or the section or sections being amended if the article being amended is divided into identified sections.
(d) A statement that the amendment or amendments were approved by the unanimous vote of all of the members entitled to vote or by a majority in interest if an operating agreement authorizes amendment of the articles of organization by majority vote.

450.4604 Restated articles of organization.

Sec. 604.

(1) A limited liability company may integrate into a single instrument the provisions of its articles of organization that are then in effect and operative by filing restated articles of organization executed as provided in section 103.
(2) A limited liability company may include amendments to its articles of organization in restated articles of organization filed under subsection (1). An amendment to the articles of organization of a limited liability company in connection with the integration and restatement of the articles under this section is subject to any other provision of this act that would apply if a certificate of amendment were filed to effect the amendment, including the requirement of member approval.
(3) A limited liability company shall specifically designate restated articles of organization filed under this section as such in the heading and shall state, either in the heading or in an introductory paragraph, the present name of the limited liability company, all of the former names of the limited liability company if the name has changed, and the date of filing of its original articles of organization. If the restated articles include a further amendment under subsection (2), the articles shall state that the amendment was approved by 1 of the following:
    (a) If an operating agreement establishes a vote requirement for amending the articles of organization, by the vote required under the operating agreement.
    (b) If subdivision (a) does not apply, by a unanimous vote of all of the members entitled to vote on the amendment.

(4) When its restated articles of organization become effective under section 104, the limited liability company's original articles of organization are superseded and the restated articles are the articles of organization of the company.

Article 7

450.4701 Domestic limited liability companies; merger; plan.

Sec. 701.

(1) Two or more domestic limited liability companies may merge pursuant to a plan of merger approved as provided in section 702.
(2) The plan of merger shall set forth all of the following:
    (a) The name of each constituent company and the name of the surviving company.
    (b) The terms and conditions of the proposed merger, including the manner and basis of converting the membership interests in each limited liability company into membership interests in the surviving company, or into cash or other property, or into a combination thereof.
    (c) A statement of any amendment to the articles of organization of the surviving company to be effected by the merger or any restatement of the articles of organization, or a statement that no changes are to be made in the articles of organization of the surviving company.
    (d) Other provisions with respect to the proposed merger that the constituent companies consider necessary or desirable.

450.4702 Merger; approval of plan by members; withdrawal and distribution.

Sec. 702.

(1) A plan of merger shall be submitted to the members of each constituent company for approval. A unanimous vote of the members entitled to vote in each constituent company is required to approve a merger, unless an operating agreement of a constituent company provides otherwise.
(2) If an operating agreement of a constituent company provides for approval of a merger by less than unanimous vote of members entitled to vote and the merger is approved, a member that did not vote in favor of the merger may withdraw from the limited liability company and receive, within a reasonable time, the fair

value of the member's interest in the limited liability company, based upon the member's share of distributions as determined under section 303.

450.4703 Plan of merger; execution; certificate; contents and effectiveness.

Sec. 703.

(1) After a plan of merger is approved, a certificate of merger shall be executed as provided in section 103 and filed on behalf of each constituent company. The certificate shall set forth all of the following:
    (a) The statements required by section 701(2)(a) and (c).
    (b) A statement that the plan of merger has been approved by the members of the constituent company in accordance with section 702(1).
    (c) A statement of any assumed names of merging limited liability companies transferred to the surviving company as authorized by section 206(6), specifying each transferred assumed name and the name of the limited liability company from which it is transferred. The certificate may include a statement of limited liability company names or assumed names of merging limited liability companies that are to be treated as newly filed assumed names of the survivor pursuant to section 206(7).
    (d) The effective date of the merger if later than the date the certificate of merger is filed.
(2) The certificate of merger is effective in accordance with section 104.

450.4704 Merger; provisions.

Sec. 704.

When a merger takes effect, all of the following apply:

(a) Every other constituent company merges into the surviving company and the separate existence of every constituent company except the surviving company ceases.
(b) All property, real, personal, and mixed, all debts due on whatever account, including promises to make contributions, all other choses in action, and any other interest of or belonging to or due to each constituent company are vested in the surviving company without further act or deed and without reversion or impairment.

(c) The surviving company may use the name and the assumed names of any constituent company, if the filings required under section 206(6) and (7) are made.
(d) The surviving company has all of the liabilities of each constituent company.
(e) A proceeding pending against any constituent company may be continued as if the merger had not occurred or the surviving company may be substituted in the proceeding for the limited liability company whose existence ceased.
(f) The articles of organization of the surviving company are amended to the extent provided in the certificate of merger.
(g) The membership interests in each constituent company are converted into membership interests in the surviving company, cash, or other property as provided in the plan of merger.

450.4705 Merger of foreign limited liability companies with domestic limited liability companies; conditions; compliance and liability of surviving company.

Sec. 705.

(1) One or more foreign limited liability companies may merge with 1 or more domestic limited liability companies if both of the following are satisfied:
   (a) The merger is permitted by the law of the jurisdiction under whose law each foreign constituent company is organized and each foreign constituent company complies with that law in effecting the merger.
   (b) Each domestic constituent company complies with the provisions of sections 701 through 703.
(2) If the surviving company is to be governed by the laws of a jurisdiction other than this state, it shall comply with the provisions of this act with respect to foreign limited liability companies if it is to transact business in this state.
(3) The surviving company is liable for, and is subject to service of process in a proceeding in this state for the enforcement of, any obligation of a domestic constituent company, including any obligation to a member of the domestic constituent company who has dissented from the merger and withdrawn pursuant to section 702(2).

450.4705a Definitions; merger of domestic limited liability companies with business organizations.

Sec. 705a.

(1) As used in this section:

(a) "Business organization" means a domestic or foreign corporation, domestic or foreign nonprofit corporation, limited partnership, general partnership, or any other type of domestic or foreign business enterprise, incorporated or unincorporated, except a domestic limited liability company.
(b) "Entity" means a business organization or a domestic limited liability company.
(c) "Nonprofit corporation" means a corporation that, under the laws of the jurisdiction in which it was formed, is a nonprofit corporation, including, but not limited to, a corporation formed under or subject to, in whole or in part, the nonprofit corporation act, 1982 PA 162, MCL 450.2101 to 450.3192.
(d) "Obligated person" means a general partner of a limited partnership, a partner of a general partnership, or a participant in or an owner of an interest in any other type of business enterprise that, under applicable law, is generally liable for the obligations of the business enterprise.

(2) If all of the business organizations in a merger with 1 or more domestic limited liability companies are foreign limited liability companies, the merger shall comply with section 705 and not this section.

(3) Except as otherwise provided in subsection (2), 1 or more domestic limited liability companies may merge with 1 or more business organizations if all of the following requirements are satisfied:
(a) The merger is permitted under the law of the jurisdiction in which each constituent business organization is organized and each constituent business organization complies with that law in effecting the merger.
(b) Each foreign constituent business organization transacting business in this state complies with the applicable laws of this state.
(c) Each domestic limited liability company complies with this section.

(4) If 1 or more domestic limited liability companies propose to merge with 1 or more business organizations, each domestic limited liability company shall prepare a plan of merger that contains all of the following:
(a) The name of each constituent entity, the name of the surviving entity, the street address of the surviving entity's principal place of business, and the type of organization of the surviving entity.
(b) The terms and conditions of the proposed merger, including the manner and basis of converting the shares, partnership interests, membership interests, or other ownership interests of each constituent entity into

ownership interests or obligations of the surviving entity, or into cash or other consideration, which may include ownership interests or obligations of an entity not a party to the merger, or into a combination thereof.
- (c) If the surviving entity is to be a domestic limited liability company, a statement of the amendments to the articles of organization of the surviving company if the articles are changed by the merger, a restatement of the articles of organization, or a statement that the articles of organization of the surviving domestic limited liability company are unchanged.
- (d) Any other provision that the domestic limited liability company considers necessary or desirable.

(5) A constituent domestic limited liability company shall submit a plan of merger to the members for approval. A unanimous vote by the members entitled to vote in the constituent domestic limited liability company is required to approve a plan of merger unless an operating agreement of the constituent domestic limited liability company provides otherwise.

(6) If an operating agreement of a constituent domestic limited liability company provides for approval by less than unanimous vote of members entitled to vote and the merger is approved, a member that voted against the merger may withdraw from the domestic limited liability company and receive, within a reasonable time, the fair value of the member's interest in the domestic limited liability company, based on the member's share of distributions as determined under section 303.

(7) If a plan of merger is approved, a certificate of merger shall be executed as provided in section 103 and filed on behalf of each constituent domestic limited liability company. The certificate of merger shall contain all of the following:
- (a) The information required under subsection (4)(a) and the statement required under subsection (4)(c).
- (b) A statement that the plan of merger was approved by the members of each constituent domestic limited liability company in accordance with subsection (5).
- (c) A statement of any assumed names of merging entities transferred to the surviving entity in accordance with section 206(6), specifying each transferred assumed name and the name of the entity from which it is transferred. If the surviving entity is a domestic limited liability company or a foreign limited liability company authorized to transact business in this state, the certificate may include a statement of 1 or more names or assumed names of merging entities that are to be treated as new certificates of assumed names of the surviving company under section 206(7).
- (d) The effective date of the merger if later than the date the certificate of merger is filed.

(8) A certificate of merger is effective in accordance with section 104.
(9) When a merger is effective under this section, all of the following apply:
- (a) Every other constituent entity merges into the surviving entity and the separate existence of every entity except the surviving entity ceases.
- (b) The title to all property, real, personal, and mixed, and rights owned by each constituent entity are vested in the surviving entity without reversion or impairment.
- (c) A surviving company may use the name and the assumed names of any merging entity if a filing required under section 206(6) or (7) or other applicable statute is made.
- (d) The surviving entity has all of the liabilities of each constituent entity. This section does not affect liability, if any, of a person that was an obligated person with respect to a merging entity for acts or omissions that occurred before the merger.
- (e) A proceeding pending against any constituent entity may be continued as if the merger did not occur or the surviving entity may be substituted in the proceeding for the entity whose existence ceased.
- (f) The articles of organization of a surviving domestic limited liability company are amended to the extent provided in the plan of merger.
- (g) The ownership interests of each constituent entity that are to be converted into ownership interests or obligations of the surviving entity or into cash or other property are converted.

(10) If the surviving entity is a foreign business organization, it is subject to the laws of this state pertaining to the transaction of business in this state by a foreign business organization if it transacts business in this state. The surviving entity is liable for, and is subject to service of process in a proceeding in this state for the enforcement of, any obligation of a constituent domestic limited liability company, including an obligation to a member of the constituent domestic limited liability company that has dissented from the merger and withdrawn in accordance with subsection (6).

450.4706 Abandoning plan of merger; procedure.

Sec. 706.

(1) Unless a plan of merger provides otherwise, at any time before the effective date of a certificate of merger, the merger may be abandoned in accordance with the procedure set forth in the plan of merger or, if no procedure to abandon the merger is set forth in the plan of merger, by the unanimous vote of the members entitled to vote in each domestic limited liability company that is

a constituent entity, unless an operating agreement of a domestic limited liability company provides otherwise.

(2) If a certificate of merger has been filed by a constituent domestic limited liability company, it shall file a certificate of abandonment within 10 days after the abandonment but not later than the effective date of the certificate of merger.

450.4707 Conversion of domestic partnership or domestic limited partnership to limited liability company.

Sec. 707.

(1) A domestic partnership or domestic limited partnership may convert to a limited liability company in accordance with this section.

(2) The terms and conditions of a conversion under this section shall be approved by the partners in the manner provided in the partnership agreement for amendments to the partnership agreement or, if no provision for amendments to the partnership agreement is made in the partnership agreement, by all of the partners.

(3) If a conversion under this section is approved, the converting partnership or limited partnership shall file both of the following:
 (a) Articles of organization that comply with section 203.
 (b) A certificate of conversion, stating the name of the partnership or limited partnership and the date it was formed. In the case of a limited partnership, the certificate of conversion shall include a statement that the certificate of limited partnership is canceled as of the effective date of the articles of organization.

(4) If a limited partnership converts to a limited liability company under this section, the certificate of limited partnership is canceled as of the effective date of the articles of organization.

(5) If a conversion under this section takes effect, the limited liability company is considered the same entity that existed before the conversion. All property and rights of the converting partnership or limited partnership remain vested in the converted limited liability company. All liabilities of the converting partnership or limited partnership continue as liabilities of the converted limited liability company. An action or proceeding pending against the converting partnership or limited partnership may be continued as if the conversion under this section had not occurred. The liability, if any, of a general partner of the converting partnership or limited partnership for acts or omissions that occurred before a conversion under this section is not affected by a conversion under this section.

450.4708 Conversion into business organization; requirements; effectiveness of certificate of conversion; foreign business organization as surviving business organization; "business organization" and "entity" defined.

Sec. 708.

(1) A domestic limited liability company may convert into a business organization if all of the following requirements are satisfied:
  (a) The conversion is permitted by the law that will govern the internal affairs of the business organization after conversion and the surviving business organization complies with that law in converting.
  (b) Unless subdivision (d) applies, the domestic limited liability company proposing to convert adopts a plan of conversion that includes all of the following:
    (i) The name of the domestic limited liability company, the name of the business organization into which the domestic limited liability company is converting, the type of business organization into which the domestic limited liability company is converting, identification of the statute that will govern the internal affairs of the surviving business organization, the street address of the surviving business organization, the street address of the domestic limited liability company if different from the street address of the surviving business organization, and the principal place of business of the surviving business organization.
    (ii) The terms and conditions of the proposed conversion, including the manner and basis of converting the membership interests of the domestic limited liability company into ownership interests or obligations of the surviving business organization, into cash, into other consideration that may include ownership interests or obligations of an entity that is not a party to the conversion, or into a combination of cash and other consideration.
    (iii) The terms and conditions of the organizational documents that are to govern the surviving business organization.
    (iv) Any other provisions with respect to the proposed conversion that the domestic limited liability company considers necessary or desirable.
  (c) A vote of the members of a domestic limited liability company is required to adopt a plan of conversion under subdivision (b). A unanimous vote of the members

entitled to vote is required to approve a plan of conversion unless the articles of organization or an operating agreement provide otherwise. If the articles of organization or an operating agreement of the domestic limited liability company provide for approval by less than a unanimous vote of members entitled to vote and the conversion is approved, a member that did not vote in favor of the conversion may withdraw from the domestic limited liability company before the conversion and receive, within a reasonable time, the fair value of the member's interest in the domestic limited liability company.

(d) If the domestic limited liability company has not commenced business; has not issued any membership interests; has no debts or other liabilities; and has not received any payments, or has returned any payments it has received after deducting any amount disbursed for payment of expenses, for subscriptions for its membership interests, subdivisions (b) and (c) do not apply and the organizers of the domestic limited liability company may approve of the conversion of the domestic limited liability company into a business organization by unanimous consent. To effect the conversion, a majority of the organizers must execute and file a certificate of conversion under subdivision (e).

(e) If the plan of conversion is approved under subdivision (c) or the conversion is approved under subdivision (d), the domestic limited liability company files any formation documents required to be filed under the laws governing the internal affairs of the surviving business organization, in the manner prescribed by those laws, and files a certificate of conversion with the administrator. The certificate of conversion shall include all of the following:
    (i) Unless subdivision (d) applies, all of the information described in subdivision (b)(i).
    (ii) A statement that the members of the domestic limited liability company have adopted the plan of conversion under subdivision (c), or that the organizers of the domestic limited liability company have approved of the conversion under subdivision (d), as applicable.
    (iii) A statement that the surviving business organization will furnish a copy of the plan of conversion, on request and without cost, to any member of the domestic limited liability company.
    (iv) A statement specifying each assumed name of the domestic limited liability company that the

surviving business organization is authorized to continue to use under section 206(8).

(2) Section 104 applies in determining when a certificate of conversion under this section becomes effective.

(3) When a conversion under this section takes effect, all of the following apply:

(a) The domestic limited liability company converts into the surviving business organization, and the articles of organization of the domestic limited liability company are canceled. Except as otherwise provided in this section, the surviving business organization is organized under and subject to the organizational laws of the jurisdiction of the surviving business organization as stated in the certificate of conversion.

(b) The surviving business organization has all of the liabilities of the domestic limited liability company. The conversion of the domestic limited liability company into a business organization under this section shall not be considered to affect any obligations or liabilities of the domestic limited liability company incurred before the conversion or the personal liability of any person incurred before the conversion, and the conversion shall not be considered to affect the choice of law applicable to the domestic limited liability company with respect to matters arising before the conversion.

(c) The title to all real estate and other property and rights owned by the domestic limited liability company remain vested in the surviving business organization without reversion or impairment. The rights, privileges, powers, and interests in property of the domestic limited liability company, as well as the debts, liabilities, and duties of the domestic limited liability company, shall not be considered, as a consequence of the conversion, to have been transferred to the surviving business organization to which the domestic limited liability company has converted for any purpose of the laws of this state.

(d) The surviving business organization may use the name and the assumed names of the domestic limited liability company if the filings required under section 206(8) or any other applicable statute are made and the laws regarding use and form of names are followed.

(e) A proceeding pending against the domestic limited liability company may be continued as if the conversion had not occurred, or the surviving business organization may be substituted in the proceeding for the domestic limited liability company.

(f) The surviving business organization is considered to be the same entity that existed before the conversion and is considered to be organized on the date that the domestic limited liability company was originally organized.

(g) The membership interests of the domestic limited liability company that were to be converted into ownership interests or obligations of the surviving business organization or into cash or other property are converted.

(h) Unless otherwise provided in a plan of conversion adopted in accordance with this section, the domestic limited liability company is not required to wind up its affairs or pay its liabilities and distribute its assets on account of the conversion, and the conversion does not constitute a dissolution of the domestic limited liability company.

(4) If the surviving business organization of a conversion under this section is a foreign business organization, it is subject to the laws of this state pertaining to the transaction of business in this state if it transacts business in this state. The surviving business organization is liable for, and is subject to service of process in a proceeding in this state for the enforcement of, an obligation of the domestic limited liability company, and in a proceeding for the enforcement of a right of a member of the domestic limited liability company that has withdrawn under subsection (1)(c).

(5) As used in this section and section 709, "business organization" and "entity" mean those terms as defined in section 705a.

450.4709 Conversion of business organization into domestic limited liability company; requirements; effectiveness of certificate of conversion.

Sec. 709.

(1) A business organization may convert into a domestic limited liability company if all of the following requirements are satisfied:
  (a) The conversion is permitted by the law that governs the internal affairs of the business organization, and the business organization complies with that law in converting.
  (b) The business organization proposing to convert into a domestic limited liability company adopts a plan of conversion that includes all of the following:
    (i) The name of the business organization, the type of business organization that is converting, identification of the statute that governs the internal affairs of the business organization, the name of the surviving domestic limited liability company into which the business organization is converting, the street address of the surviving domestic limited liability company, the street

address of the business organization if different from the street address of the surviving domestic limited liability company, and the principal place of business of the surviving domestic limited liability company.
  (ii) The terms and conditions of the proposed conversion, including the manner and basis of converting the ownership interests of the business organization into membership interests of the surviving domestic limited liability company, into cash, into other consideration that may include ownership interests or obligations of an entity that is not a party to the conversion, or into a combination of cash and other consideration.
  (iii) The terms and conditions of the articles of organization that are to govern the surviving domestic limited liability company.
  (iv) Any other provisions with respect to the proposed conversion that the business organization considers necessary or desirable.
(c) If a plan of conversion is adopted by the business organization under subdivision (b), the plan of conversion is submitted for approval in the manner required by the law governing the internal affairs of that business organization.
(d) If the plan of conversion is approved under subdivisions (b) and (c), the business organization executes as provided in section 103 and files a certificate of conversion with the administrator. The certificate of conversion shall include all of the following:
  (i) All of the information described in subdivision (b)(i) and (ii).
  (ii) A statement that the business organization has obtained approval of the plan of conversion under subdivision (c).
  (iii) A statement that the surviving domestic limited liability company will furnish a copy of the plan of conversion, on request and without cost, to any owner of the business organization.
  (iv) A statement specifying each assumed name of the business organization that the surviving domestic limited liability company is authorized to continue to use under section 206(9).
  (v) Articles of organization for the surviving domestic limited liability company that meet all of the requirements of this act applicable to articles of organization.

(2) Section 104 applies in determining when a certificate of conversion under this section becomes effective.
(3) When a conversion under this section takes effect, all of the following apply:
  (a) The business organization converts into the surviving domestic limited liability company. Except as otherwise provided in this section, the surviving domestic limited liability company is organized under and subject to this act.
  (b) The surviving domestic limited liability company has all of the liabilities of the business organization. The conversion of the business organization into a domestic limited liability company under this section shall not be considered to affect any obligations or liabilities of the business organization incurred before the conversion or the personal liability of any person incurred before the conversion, and the conversion shall not be considered to affect the choice of law applicable to the business organization with respect to matters arising before the conversion.
  (c) The title to all real estate and other property and rights owned by the business organization remains vested in the surviving domestic limited liability company without reversion or impairment. The rights, privileges, powers, and interests in property of the business organization, as well as the debts, liabilities, and duties of the business organization, shall not be considered, as a consequence of the conversion, to have been transferred to the surviving domestic limited liability company to which the business organization has converted for any purpose of the laws of this state.
  (d) The surviving domestic limited liability company may use the name and the assumed names of the business organization if the filings required under section 206(9) or any other applicable statute are made and the laws regarding use and form of names are followed.
  (e) A proceeding pending against the business organization may be continued as if the conversion had not occurred, or the surviving domestic limited liability company may be substituted in the proceeding for the business organization.
  (f) The surviving domestic limited liability company is considered to be the same entity that existed before the conversion and is considered to be organized on the date that the business organization was originally organized.
  (g) The ownership interests of the business organization that were to be converted into membership interests or obligations of the surviving domestic limited liability company or into cash or other property are converted.

51

(h) Unless otherwise provided in a plan of conversion adopted in accordance with this section, the business organization is not required to wind up its affairs or pay its liabilities and distribute its assets on account of the conversion, and the conversion does not constitute a dissolution of the business organization.

Article 8

450.4801 Dissolution and winding up; conditions.

Sec. 801.

A limited liability company is dissolved and its affairs shall be wound up when the first of the following occurs:
(a) Automatically, if a time specified in the articles of organization is reached.
(b) If a vote of the members or other event specified in the articles of organization or in an operating agreement takes place.
(c) The members entitled to vote unanimously vote for dissolution.
(d) Automatically, if a decree of judicial dissolution is entered.
(e) A majority of the organizers of the limited liability company vote for dissolution, if the limited liability company has not commenced business; has not issued any membership interests; has no debts or other liabilities; and has not received any payments, or has returned any payments it has received after deducting any amount disbursed for payment of expenses, for subscriptions for its membership interests.

450.4802 Dissolution; decree by circuit court.

Sec. 802.

Upon application by or for a member, the circuit court for the county in which the registered office of a limited liability company is located may decree dissolution of the company whenever the company is unable to carry on business in conformity with the articles of organization or operating agreements.

450.4803 Dissolution; action by attorney general; grounds; other actions not excluded.

Sec. 803.

(1) The attorney general may bring an action in the circuit court for the county in which the registered office of a limited liability

company is located for dissolution of the limited liability company on the ground that the company has committed any of the following acts:
- (a) Procured its organization through fraud.
- (b) Repeatedly and willfully exceeded the authority conferred on it by law.
- (c) Repeatedly and willfully conducted its business in an unlawful manner.
- (d) If the limited liability company is a low-profit limited liability company, ceased to meet any of the requirements described in section 102(m) and for 60 days after it ceased to meet those requirements failed to file a certificate of amendment amending its name to conform with the requirements of section 204.

(2) This section does not exclude any other statutory or common law action by the attorney general for dissolution of a limited liability company.

450.4804 Certificate of dissolution; filing; contents.

Sec. 804.

(1) When it begins winding up its affairs, a limited liability company that dissolves under section 801(b) or (c) shall execute a certificate of dissolution as provided in section 103 and file the certificate with the administrator. The certificate of dissolution shall contain all of the following:
- (a) The name of the limited liability company.
- (b) The reason for the dissolution.
- (c) The effective date of the dissolution if later than the date of filing of the certificate of dissolution.

(2) When it begins winding up its affairs, a limited liability company that dissolves under section 801(e) shall execute a certificate of dissolution as provided in section 103 and file the certificate with the administrator. The certificate of dissolution shall contain all of the following:
- (a) The name of the limited liability company.
- (b) A statement that includes all of the following:
  - (i) That the limited liability company has not commenced business, has not issued any membership interests, and has no debts or other liabilities.
  - (ii) That the limited liability company has not received any payments, or has returned any payments it has received after deducting any amount disbursed for payment of expenses, for subscriptions for its membership interests.
  - (iii) That a majority of the organizers of the limited liability company have approved the dissolution.

450.4805 Winding up by managers, members, or circuit court; procedures; right to maintain actions.

Sec. 805.

(1) Except as otherwise provided in the articles of organization, an operating agreement, or this section, the members or managers that have not wrongfully dissolved a limited liability company may wind up the company's affairs, but the circuit court for the county in which the registered office is located may wind up the limited liability company's affairs on application of, and for good cause shown by, any member or legal representative or assignee of a member.
(2) The members or managers that are winding up a limited liability company's affairs shall continue to function, for the purpose of winding up, in accordance with the procedures established by this act, the articles of organization, and operating agreements, shall not be held to a greater standard of conduct than that described in section 404, and are not subject to any greater liabilities than would apply in the absence of dissolution.
(3) A dissolved limited liability company may sue and be sued in its name and process may issue by and against the company in the same manner as if dissolution had not occurred. An action brought by or against a limited liability company before its dissolution does not abate because of the dissolution.

450.4806 Dissolution; notice to existing claimants; contents; validity of claim not recognized; claims barred under certain conditions; "existing claim" defined; effective date of notice.

Sec. 806.

(1) The dissolved limited liability company may notify its existing claimants in writing of the dissolution at any time after the effective date of the dissolution. The written notice shall include all of the following:
    (a) A description of the information that must be included in a claim. The limited liability company may demand sufficient information to permit it to make a reasonable judgment whether the claim should be accepted or rejected.
    (b) A mailing address where a claim may be sent.
    (c) The deadline, which may not be less than 6 months after the effective date of the written notice, by which the dissolved limited liability company must receive the claim.
    (d) A statement that the claim will be barred if not received by the deadline.

(2) The giving of notice provided for in subsection (1) does not constitute recognition that a person to whom the notice is directed has a valid claim against the limited liability company.
(3) A claim against the dissolved limited liability company is barred if either of the following applies:
- (a) If a claimant who was given written notice under subsection (1) does not deliver the claim to the dissolved limited liability company by the deadline.
- (b) If a claimant whose claim was rejected by a written notice of rejection by the dissolved limited liability company does not commence a proceeding to enforce the claim within 90 days after the effective date of the written notice of rejection.

(4) For purposes of this section and section 807, "existing claim" means any claim or right against the limited liability company, liquidated or unliquidated. "Existing claim" does not mean a contingent liability or a claim based on an event occurring after the effective date of dissolution.
(5) For purposes of this section, the effective date of the written notice is the earliest of the following:
- (a) The date it is received.
- (b) Five days after its deposit in the United States mail, as evidenced by the postmark, if it is mailed postpaid and correctly addressed.
- (c) The date shown on the return receipt, if the notice is sent by registered or certified mail, return receipt requested, and the receipt is signed by or on behalf of the addressee.

450.4807 Dissolution; publication of notice; requirements; commencing proceeding to enforce claims; claimants with known existing claims not receiving notice.

Sec. 807.

(1) A dissolved limited liability company may also publish notice of dissolution and request that persons with claims against the company present them in accordance with the notice.
(2) The notice shall be in accord with all the following:
- (a) Be published 1 time in a newspaper of general circulation in the county in which the dissolved limited liability company's principal place of business, or if none in this state, its registered office, is or was located.
- (b) Describe the information that must be included in a claim and provide a mailing address where the claim may be sent. The limited liability company may demand sufficient information to permit it to make a reasonable judgment whether the claim should be accepted or rejected.

(c) State that a claim against the limited liability company will be barred unless a proceeding to enforce the claim is commenced within 1 year after the publication date of the newspaper notice.

(3) If the dissolved limited liability company publishes a newspaper notice in accordance with subsection (2), the claim of each of the following claimants is barred unless the claimant commences a proceeding to enforce the claim against the dissolved company within 1 year after the publication date of the newspaper:
(a) A claimant who did not receive written notice under section 806.
(b) A claimant whose claim was timely sent to the dissolved limited liability company but not acted on.
(c) A claimant whose claim is contingent or based on an event occurring after the effective date of dissolution.

(4) Notwithstanding subsection (3), a claimant having an existing claim known to the limited liability company at the time of publication in accordance with subsection (2) and who did not receive written notice under section 806 is not barred from suit until 6 months after the claimant has actual notice of the dissolution.

450.4808 Winding up; distribution of assets; order; filing tax returns and paying tax obligations.

Sec. 808.

(1) Upon the winding up of a limited liability company, the assets shall be distributed in the following order:
(a) To creditors, including members who are creditors, to the extent permitted by law, in satisfaction of liabilities of the limited liability company other than liabilities for distributions to members under section 304 or 305. Reasonable provision shall be made for debts, liabilities, and obligations that are not liquidated but will not be barred under section 806 or 807.
(b) Except as provided in an operating agreement, to members and former members in satisfaction of liabilities for distributions under sections 304 and 305.
(c) Except as provided in an operating agreement, all remaining assets to members and former members in accordance with their shares of distributions as determined under section 303.

(2) Before the assets of a limited liability company are distributed pursuant to subsection (1), the limited liability company shall file tax returns and pay tax obligations as required by Act No. 122 of the Public Acts of 1941, being sections 205.1 to 205.31 of the Michigan Compiled Laws.

Article 9

450.4901 Limited liability company; rendering professional services; applicability of article.

Sec. 901.

(1) A limited liability company formed to render 1 or more professional services, as defined in section 902 may be organized under this article as a professional limited liability company.
(2) A limited liability company formed as a professional limited liability company and its members and managers are subject to this article and this act. This article takes precedence over any other provision of this act in the event of conflict.

450.4902 Definitions.

Sec. 902.

As used in this article:

(a) "Licensed person" means an individual who is licensed or otherwise legally authorized to practice a professional service by a court, department, board, commission, or an agency of this state or another jurisdiction, any corporation or professional services corporation all of whose shareholders are licensed persons, any partnership all of whose partners are licensed persons, or any limited liability company all of whose members and managers are licensed persons.
(b) "Professional service" means a type of personal service to the public that requires as a condition precedent to the rendering of the service the obtaining of a license or other legal authorization. Professional service includes, but is not limited to, services rendered by a certified or other public accountant, chiropractor, dentist, optometrist, veterinarian, osteopathic physician, physician, surgeon, podiatrist, chiropodist, physician's assistant, architect, professional engineer, land surveyor, or attorney-at-law.
(c) "Professional services corporation" means a corporation formed under former 1962 PA 192 or a corporation incorporated under and governed by chapter 2A of the business corporation act, 1972 PA 284, MCL 450.1101 to 450.2098.

450.4903 Professional limited liability company; purpose stated in articles of organization; name.

Sec. 903.

(1) One or more licensed persons may organize and become members of a professional limited liability company.
(2) The articles of organization of a professional limited liability company shall state, as its purposes, that the company is formed to render specified professional services.
(3) The name of the limited liability company shall contain the words "professional limited liability company" or the abbreviation "P.L.L.C." or "P.L.C." with or without periods or other punctuation.

450.4904 Rendering professional services; organization of professional liability company or professional limited liability company; license or legal authorization of persons required.

Sec. 904.

(1) Except as provided in this section or otherwise prohibited, a professional limited liability company may render 1 or more professional services, and each member and manager must be a licensed person in 1 or more of the professional services rendered by the company.
(2) Except as provided in subsection (3) or (4), if a professional limited liability company renders a professional service that is included within the public health code, 1978 PA 368, MCL 333.1101 to 333.25211, then all members and managers of the company must be licensed or legally authorized in this state to render the same professional service.
(3) One or more individuals licensed to engage in the practice of medicine under part 170, the practice of osteopathic medicine and surgery under part 175, or the practice of podiatric medicine and surgery under part 180 of article 15 of the public health code, 1978 PA 368, MCL 333.16101 to 333.18838, may organize a professional liability company under this article with 1 or more other individuals licensed to engage in the practice of medicine under part 170, the practice of osteopathic medicine and surgery under part 175, or the practice of podiatric medicine and surgery under part 180 of article 15 of the public health code, 1978 PA 368, MCL 333.16101 to 333.18838.
(4) Subject to section 17048 of the public health code, 1978 PA 368, MCL 333.17048, 1 or more individuals licensed to engage in the practice of medicine under part 170, the practice of osteopathic medicine and surgery under part 175, or the practice of podiatric medicine and surgery under part 180 of article 15 of the public

health code, 1978 PA 368, MCL 333.16101 to 333.18838, may organize a professional limited liability company under this article with 1 or more physician's assistants licensed under article 15 of the public health code, 1978 PA 368, MCL 333.16101 to 333.18838. Beginning on July 19, 2010, 1 or more physician's assistants may not organize a professional limited liability company under this act that will have only physician's assistants as members.

(5) A licensed person of another jurisdiction may become a member, manager, employee, or agent of a professional limited liability company, but shall not render any professional services in this state until the person is licensed or otherwise legally authorized to render the professional service in this state.

(6) A limited liability company may engage in the practice of architecture, professional engineering, or professional surveying in this state if not less than 2/3 of the members or managers of the limited liability company are licensed in this state to render 1 or more of the professional services offered. A professional limited liability company organized under this article may engage in the practice of architecture, professional engineering, or professional surveying in this state if all of the members and managers of the professional limited liability company organized under this article are licensed in this state to render 1 or more of the professional services offered.

(7) A professional limited liability company organized under this article may engage in the practice of public accounting, as defined in section 720 of the occupational code, 1980 PA 299, MCL 339.720, in this state if more than 50% of the equity and voting rights of the professional limited liability company are held directly or beneficially by individuals who are licensed or otherwise authorized to engage in the practice of public accounting under article 7 of the occupational code, 1980 PA 299, MCL 339.720 to 339.736.

450.4905 Professional limited liability company; license required; "employee" explained; effect of act on laws applicable to professional relationship and liabilities; liability for negligent or wrongful acts.

Sec. 905.

(1) A professional limited liability company shall not render professional services within this state except through its members, managers, employees, and agents who are licensed or otherwise legally authorized to render the professional services within this state. The term employee does not include secretaries, bookkeepers, technicians, and other assistants who are not usually and ordinarily considered by custom and practice to be

rendering professional services to the public for which a license or other legal authorization is required.

(2) This act shall not be construed to abolish, repeal, modify, restrict, or limit the law now in effect applicable to the professional relationship and liabilities between the person furnishing the professional services and the person receiving such professional services and to the standards for professional conduct. A member, manager, employee, or agent of a professional limited liability company shall remain personally and fully liable and accountable for any negligent or wrongful acts or misconduct committed by him or her, or by any person under his or her direct supervision and control, while rendering professional services on behalf of the company to the person for whom the professional services were being rendered.

(3) The limited liability company shall be liable up to the full value of its property for any negligent or wrongful acts or misconduct committed by any of its members, managers, employees, or agents while they are engaged on behalf of the company in the rendering of professional services.

450.4906 Disqualification, restriction, or limitation on persons rendering professional service; severing employment and financial interest; noncompliance.

Sec. 906.

If a member, manager, employee, or agent of a professional limited liability company becomes legally disqualified to render the professional services rendered by the company or accepts employment that, pursuant to existing law, places restrictions or limitations on his or her continued rendering of the professional services, he or she shall sever within a reasonable period all employment with and financial interests in the company. A company's failure to require compliance with this section constitutes a ground for the forfeiture of its articles of organization and its dissolution. If a company's failure to comply with this section is brought to the attention of the administrator, he or she shall certify that fact to the attorney general for appropriate action to dissolve the company.

450.4907 Professional limited liability company; prohibited activities; exception.

Sec. 907.

(1) A professional limited liability company shall not engage in any business other than the rendering of the professional services for which it was specifically organized.

(2) This act does not prohibit the company from investing its funds in real estate, mortgages, stocks, bonds, or any other type of investments, owning real or personal property necessary for the rendering of professional services, becoming a partner in a partnership formed under Act No. 72 of the Public Acts of 1917, being sections 449.1 to 449.43 of the Michigan Compiled Laws, if the partnership performs the same professional services as the professional limited liability company, or forming or becoming a member or manager of another professional limited liability company organized under this act if both professional limited liability companies perform the same professional services.

450.4908 Sale or transfer of membership interest; restrictions.

Sec. 908.

(1) A membership interest in a professional limited liability company shall not be sold or transferred except to a person who is eligible to be a member of the company or to the personal representative or estate of a deceased or legally incompetent member. The personal representative or estate of the member may continue to hold a membership interest for a reasonable period but shall not be authorized to participate in any decisions concerning the rendering of professional service.
(2) The articles of organization or an operating agreement may provide specifically for additional restrictions on the transfer of membership interests.

450.4909 Annual report; filing fee; penalty for late filing.

Sec. 909.

(1) In addition to the annual statement required in section 207(3), a professional limited liability company shall file with the administrator an annual report, together with a $50.00 filing fee, listing the names and addresses of all members and managers and certifying that each member and manager is a licensed person in 1 or more of the professional services rendered by the company. The report shall also certify that any member or manager not licensed or otherwise legally authorized to render professional services in this state does not render professional services in this state.
(2) The professional limited liability company shall file the annual report not later than February 15 of each year, and a penalty of $50.00 shall be added to the fee if the annual report is not filed or the fee is not paid by February 15, except that if a professional limited liability company is formed after September 30, it need

not file an annual report on the February 15 immediately succeeding its formation.

(3) If a professional limited liability company fails to file an annual report required by this section for 2 consecutive years, the administrator shall notify the company of the consequences of the failure to file under subsection (4).

(4) If a professional limited liability company does not file all annual reports it has failed to file, the applicable fees, and the penalty described in subsection (2) within 60 days after the administrator's notice under subsection (3) is sent, the professional limited liability company is not in good standing. A professional limited liability company that is not in good standing is not entitled to issuance by the administrator of a certificate of good standing described in section 207a, the name of the company is available for use by another entity filing with the administrator, and the administrator shall not accept for filing any document submitted by the professional limited liability company other than a certificate of restoration of good standing provided for in subsection (5). A professional limited liability company that is not in good standing remains in existence and may continue to transact business in this state.

(5) A professional limited liability company that is not in good standing under subsection (4) may file a certificate of restoration of good standing, accompanied by the annual reports and fees for all of the years for which they were not filed and paid, the penalty described in subsection (2), and the fee for filing the certificate of restoration of good standing. The certificate shall include all of the following:
  (a) The name of the professional limited liability company at the time it ceased to be in good standing. If that name is not available when the certificate of restoration of good standing is filed, the professional limited liability company shall select a new name that complies with this act. The new name shall be the name of the professional limited liability company from the date of filing of the certificate.
  (b) The name of the professional limited liability company's current resident agent and the address of the current registered office in this state.
  (c) A statement that the certificate is accompanied by the annual reports and applicable fees for all of the years for which reports were not filed and fees were not paid and the penalty described in subsection (2).

(6) A professional limited liability company that fails to file annual statements under section 207 as well as annual reports under this section must comply with section 207a and this section to maintain or restore its good standing.

450.4910 Merger; limitation.

Sec. 910.

A professional limited liability company may merge only with other limited liability companies whose members and managers are licensed persons permitted to be members or managers under this article or other entities that are licensed persons or whose shareholders, partners, or other owners, members, or managers are licensed persons permitted to be members or managers under this article.

Article 10

450.5001 Foreign limited liability company; laws of jurisdiction.

Sec. 1001.

Subject to the constitution of this state, the laws of the jurisdiction under which a foreign limited liability company is organized shall govern its organization and internal affairs, and a foreign limited liability company shall not be denied a certificate of authority to transact business in this state by reason of any difference between those laws and the laws of this state.

450.5002 Transacting business; certificate of authority by foreign limited liability company required; application; filing; contents.

Sec. 1002.

Before transacting business in this state, a foreign limited liability company shall obtain a certificate of authority from the administrator. To obtain a certificate of authority, a foreign limited liability company shall file with the administrator an application, executed as provided in section 103, setting forth all of the following:
(a) The name of the foreign limited liability company and, if different, the name under which it proposes to transact business in this state.
(b) The jurisdiction and date of its organization.
(c) The address of its registered office in this state and the name of its resident agent at that address in accordance with section 207.
(d) A statement that includes both of the following:
 (i) That the department is appointed the agent of the foreign limited liability company for service of process if no agent has been appointed under subdivision (c), or, if appointed, the agent's authority has been revoked, the

agent has resigned, or the agent cannot be found or served through the exercise of reasonable diligence.
    (ii) The name and address of a member, manager, or other person to whom the administrator is to send copies of any process served on the administrator.
(e) The address of the office required to be maintained in the jurisdiction of its organization by the laws of that state or, if not required to maintain an office by the laws of that state, of the principal office of the foreign limited liability company.
(f) Other additional information as may be necessary or appropriate in order to enable the department to determine whether the limited liability company is entitled to transact business in this state.

450.5003 Certificate of authority; issuance; powers, rights, and privileges of foreign limited liability company.

Sec. 1003.

(1) If the administrator finds that an application for a certificate of authority substantially conforms to the requirements of this act and all requisite fees have been paid, the administrator shall file the application and issue to the foreign limited liability company a certificate of authority to transact business in this state, in accordance with section 104.
(2) Upon the issuance of a certificate of authority, the foreign limited liability company may transact in this state any business that a domestic limited liability company formed under this act may lawfully transact, except as limited by statements in its application for a certificate of authority or under the law of its jurisdiction of organization. The authority continues so long as the foreign limited liability company retains its authority to transact such business in the jurisdiction of its organization and its authority to transact business in this state has not been surrendered, suspended, or revoked.
(3) A foreign limited liability company holding a valid certificate of authority in this state has no greater rights or privileges than a domestic limited liability company. The certificate of authority does not authorize the foreign limited liability company to exercise any of its powers or purposes that a domestic limited liability company is forbidden by law to exercise in this state.

450.5004 Certificate of authority; satisfaction of MCL 450.4204 required for issuance.

Sec. 1004.

The department shall not issue a certificate of authority to a foreign limited liability company unless the name of the company satisfies the requirements of section 204. If the name of a foreign limited liability company does not satisfy the requirements of section 204, the company may take the action authorized by section 204(4).

450.5005 Inaccurate application; correcting statement; certificate; exception; survivor of merger; certificate attesting to merger; annual statement.

Sec. 1005.

(1) If any statement in the application for certificate of authority of a foreign limited liability company was false when made or any arrangements or other facts described have changed, making the application inaccurate in any respect, the foreign limited liability company shall promptly file with the administrator a certificate, signed as provided in section 103, correcting the statement, except that a change in the resident agent or registered office may be made under section 209.

(2) If a foreign limited liability company authorized to transact business in this state is the survivor of a merger permitted by the laws of the jurisdiction of its organization, the foreign limited liability company shall file, not later than 30 days after the merger becomes effective, a certificate issued by the proper officer of the jurisdiction of its organization attesting to the occurrence of the merger. If the merger has changed the name of the foreign limited liability company or has otherwise affected the information set forth in the application, the foreign company shall also comply with subsection (1).

(3) A foreign limited liability company authorized to transact business in this state shall file an annual statement as required by section 207(3), and section 207a applies to the good standing of the company and to failures to file.

450.5006 Certificate of withdrawal; contents, form, manner, and execution of application.

Sec. 1006.

(1) A foreign limited liability company authorized to transact business in this state may withdraw from this state upon receiving from the administrator a certificate of withdrawal. In

order to obtain the certificate, the foreign limited liability company shall file an application for withdrawal setting forth all of the following:
- (a) The name of the foreign limited liability company and the jurisdiction under the laws of which it is organized.
- (b) That the foreign limited liability company is not transacting business in this state.
- (c) That the foreign limited liability company surrenders its authority to transact business in this state.
- (d) That the foreign limited liability company revokes the authority of its resident agent to receive service of process in this state and consents that service of process in any action, suit, or proceeding based upon any cause of action arising in this state during the time the foreign limited liability company was authorized to transact business in this state may thereafter be made on the company by service upon the administrator.
- (e) An address to which the administrator is to mail a copy of any process against the foreign limited liability company.
- (f) Other additional information as is necessary or appropriate in order to enable the administrator to determine and assess any unpaid fees payable by the foreign limited liability company.

(2) The application for withdrawal shall be in the form and manner designated by the administrator and shall be executed for the foreign limited liability company as provided in section 103, or, if the foreign limited liability company is in the hands of a receiver or trustee, by the receiver or trustee on behalf of the company.

450.5007 Foreign limited liability company; transacting business without certificate of authority.

Sec. 1007.

(1) A foreign limited liability company transacting business in this state without a certificate of authority shall not maintain an action, suit, or proceeding in a court of this state until it has obtained a certificate of authority. This prohibition applies to both of the following in addition to the foreign limited liability company:
- (a) A successor in interest of the foreign limited liability company, except a receiver, trustee in bankruptcy, or other representative of creditors of the foreign company.
- (b) An assignee of the foreign limited liability company, except an assignee for value who accepts an assignment without knowledge that the foreign company should have but has not obtained a certificate of authority in this state.

(2) An action commenced by a foreign limited liability company having no certificate of authority shall not be dismissed if a certificate of authority is obtained before the order of dismissal. Any order of dismissal shall be without prejudice to the recommencement of the action, suit, or proceeding by the foreign limited liability company after it obtains a certificate of authority.
(3) The failure of a foreign limited liability company to obtain a certificate of authority to transact business in this state does not impair the validity of any contract or act of the foreign limited liability company or prevent the foreign limited liability company from defending any action, suit, or proceeding in a court of this state.
(4) A foreign limited liability company, by transacting business in this state without a certificate of authority, appoints the administrator as its agent for service of process with respect to a cause of action arising out of the transaction of business in this state.
(5) A foreign limited liability company that transacts business in this state without a certificate of authority is liable to the state for the years or parts of years during which it transacted business in this state without a certificate in an amount equal to all fees that would have been imposed under this act upon the foreign limited liability company had it obtained the certificate, filed all documents required by this act, and paid all penalties imposed by this act. The attorney general may bring proceedings to recover all amounts due the state under this section.
(6) A foreign limited liability company that transacts business in this state without a certificate of authority is subject to a civil penalty, payable to the state, of not less than $100.00 nor more than $1,000.00 for each calendar month, not more than 5 years prior to the imposition of the penalty, in which it has transacted business without the certificate. The penalty shall not exceed $10,000.00. Each manager, member, or authorized person who authorizes, directs, or participates in the transaction of business in this state on behalf of a foreign limited liability company that does not have a certificate is subject to a civil penalty, payable to the state, not to exceed $10,000.00.
(7) The civil penalties set forth in subsection (6) may be recovered in an action brought by the attorney general. Upon a finding by the court that a foreign limited liability company or any of its members, managers, or authorized persons have transacted business in this state in violation of this act, the court shall issue, in addition to the imposition of a civil penalty, an injunction restraining the further transaction of business by the foreign limited liability company and the further exercise of any rights and privileges in this state. The foreign limited liability company shall be enjoined from transacting business in this state until all civil penalties plus any interest and court costs that the court may assess have been paid and until the foreign limited liability

company has obtained a certificate of authority to transact business.

(8) A member of a foreign limited liability company is not liable for the debts and obligations of the limited liability company solely by reason of the company's having transacted business in this state without a valid certificate of authority.

450.5008 Activities not considered to be transacting business in state; applicability of section to other state laws.

Sec. 1008.

(1) Without excluding other activities that may not constitute transacting business in this state, a foreign limited liability company is not considered to be transacting business in this state, for the purposes of this act, because it is carrying on in this state any 1 or more of the following activities:
    (a) Maintaining, defending, or settling any proceeding.
    (b) Holding meetings of its members or carrying on any other activities concerning its internal affairs.
    (c) Maintaining bank accounts.
    (d) Maintaining offices or agencies for the transfer, exchange, and registration of the foreign limited liability company's own securities or maintaining trustees or depositaries with respect to those securities.
    (e) Selling through independent contractors.
    (f) Soliciting or obtaining orders, whether by mail or through employees or agents or otherwise, if the orders require acceptance outside this state before they become contracts.
    (g) Creating or acquiring indebtedness, mortgages, and security interests in real or personal property.
    (h) Securing or collecting debts or enforcing mortgages and security interests in property securing the debts.
    (i) Owning, without more, real or personal property.
    (j) Conducting an isolated transaction that is completed within 30 days and that is not 1 in the course of repeated transactions of a like nature.
    (k) Transacting business in interstate commerce.
(2) This section does not apply in determining the contacts or activities that may subject a foreign limited liability company to service of process or taxation in this state or to regulation under any other law of this state.

450.5009 Making or purchasing loans or participation or interest in loans.

Sec. 1009.

(1) A foreign limited liability company may acquire or, through another person entitled to transact business in this state, may make loans, or participations or interests in loans, insured or guaranteed in whole or in part by the federal housing administration or the veterans' administration or a successor or similar agency of the federal government, which are secured in whole or in part by mortgages of real property located in this state, and a foreign limited liability company may purchase a loan, or participation or interest in a loan, secured in whole or in part by a mortgage of real property located in this state, without maintaining authority to transact business in this state under this act or any other law of this state relating to the qualification or authority and without paying fees as required by law.
(2) Neither the failure of a foreign limited liability company to qualify or maintain authority to transact business in this state under this act or any other law of this state nor its failure to pay fees as required by law affects or impairs its ownership of the loans or participation or interests in the loans, whether made or acquired, or its right to collect and service the loans through another person entitled to transact business in this state, or its right to enforce the loans or to acquire, hold, protect, convey, lease, and otherwise contract and deal with respect to the property mortgaged as security.

450.5010 Maintaining action to restrain by attorney general.

Sec. 1010.

The attorney general may maintain an action to restrain a foreign limited liability company transacting business in this state, with or without a certificate of authority, from any violation of this act.

Article 11

450.5101 Filing fees; use; charges for certifying or copying files or records; dishonored checks; payment by credit card; waiver.

Sec. 1101.

(1) The fees to be paid to the administrator when the documents described in this subsection are delivered to him or her for filing are as follows:
    (a) Certificate of correction, $25.00.
    (b) Articles of organization, $50.00.
    (c) Amendment to the articles of organization, $25.00.
    (d) Restated articles of organization, $50.00.
    (e) Application for reservation of name, $25.00.
    (f) Certificate of assumed name or a certificate of termination of assumed name, $25.00.
    (g) Annual statement of resident agent and registered office, $15.00 if paid through September 30, 2003 and after September 30, 2015. Beginning October 1, 2003 through September 30, 2015, the fee is $25.00.
    (h) Certificate of restoration of good standing, $50.00.
    (i) Notice of resignation of resident agent, or statement of change of registered office or resident agent, $5.00.
    (j) Certificate of merger as provided in article 7, $100.00.
    (k) Certificate of abandonment, $10.00.
    (l) Certificate of conversion, $25.00.
    (m) Certificate of dissolution, $10.00.
    (n) Application of a foreign limited liability company for a certificate of authority to transact business in this state, $50.00.
    (o) Certificate correcting statement contained in an application for a certificate of authority to transact business in this state, $25.00.
    (p) Certificate attesting to the occurrence of a merger of a foreign limited liability company, as provided in section 1005, $10.00.
    (q) Application for withdrawal and issuance of a certificate of withdrawal of a foreign limited liability company, $10.00.

(2) In addition to a fee required to file a document, the administrator may charge a fee of $50.00 if the document is filed by facsimile or other electronic transmission or the administrator is requested to transmit a document by facsimile or other electronic transmission.

(3) The administrator shall not refund all or any part of a fee described in this section. The administrator shall deposit all fees received and collected under this section in the state treasury to the credit of the administrator, who may only use the money credited pursuant to legislative appropriation and only in carrying out those duties of the department required by law.

(4) A minimum charge of $1.00 for each certificate and 50 cents per folio shall be paid to the administrator for certifying a part of a file or record pertaining to a domestic or foreign limited liability company if a fee is not set forth in subsection (1). The administrator may furnish copies of documents, reports, and papers required or permitted by law to be filed with the administrator, and shall charge for those copies pursuant to a schedule of fees that the administrator shall adopt with the approval of the state administrative board. The administrator shall retain the revenue collected under this subsection and use it to defray the costs of the department's copying and certifying services.

(5) If a domestic or foreign limited liability company pays fees or penalties by check and the check is dishonored, the fee is considered unpaid and the filing of all related documents will be rescinded.

(6) The administrator may accept payment by credit card, instead of cash or check, as payment of a fee under this act. The administrator shall determine which credit cards he or she shall accept for payment of a fee.

(7) The administrator shall waive any fee otherwise required under this section if a majority of the membership interests in the domestic or foreign limited liability company responsible for paying the fee are, and the domestic or foreign limited liability company provides proof satisfactory to the administrator that those interests are, held by 1 or more honorably discharged veterans of the armed forces of the United States.

450.5102 Effect of actions by legislature.

Sec. 1102.

This act may be supplemented, altered, amended, or repealed by the legislature, and every limited liability company subject to this act is bound by the changes.

450.5103 Interest as security.

Sec. 1103.

An interest in a limited liability company to which this act applies is a security to the same extent as an interest in a corporation, partnership, or limited partnership is a security.

450.5200 Effective date.

Sec. 1200.

This act shall take effect June 1, 1993.